Life Beyond Reggae Music

Life Beyond Reggae Music

The Artists We Love & Want to Know

Heather Dennis

Printed by Lightning Source
Typesetting by *www.wordzworth.com*
Cover design by Yegbeh Conteh & Heather Dennis

Contents

Autobiography

Ms. Heather Dennis was born on the Island of Jamaica on June 10, 1977 and spent her early years in Duhaney Park, a community in the capital city of Kingston. Not long after, due to family opportunity, she immigrated to the United States in 1989 at the age of 11 where she spent the rest of her formative years adapting to life in a new country and overcoming many of the challenges that came with being an immigrant. When she arrived in America, her peers were not hospitable, which is something that came as a surprise to her, knowing how multi-cultural Jamaica is. Though she experienced challenges, with some being extreme, she resolved to persevere; no one was going to get in the way of her achieving her dreams.

Ms. Dennis is a graduate of St. Johns University, where she earned an Associate's degree in Education; she later went on to earn her Bachelor of Science degree in Business Communications at Chestnut Hill College. Ms. Dennis settled in Pennsylvania, where she is raising her two beautiful daughters, Nicolette and Natalia, who inspire and motivate her every day. In fact, it was when she was at home with baby Natalia that she had the idea that she could write a book about something she loved, something that is strongly tied to her cultural heritage—reggae music! Her goal is to give reggae artists, some well-known and others still trying to make a name for themselves, a platform to share their love for reggae music and stories of their lives beyond the music mind. Her inspiration to write this book came after it dawned on her that no one had ever written a book about reggae artists collectively. She wanted to be the first to allow fans to get to know their reggae artists better outside of the normal magazine or newspaper interviews.

Apart from being the author of this book, Heather Dennis is the founder of the charity foundation Give A Little-Get A Lot "Helping Those In Need" *www.lbrmusic.org*. This foundation aims to help those in need by supporting charities that focus on children, the elderly, education, and health.

Ms. Dennis believes that giving is more important than receiving; this is a virtue that she has extended to her children by telling them that the true reward is usually within the giving. Her belief in this principle is what actually led her to start a charity of her own and a book that highlights the reggae artists' cause. Embracing the giving principle has brought her to the realization that her way of life may be different from others yet, she believes in what she speaks. She is an ardent believer in God and the blessings that are rewarded to those who grasp the principle of giving without expecting anything in return.

How Reggae Has Changed Over The Years

Since its founding in the late 60's, reggae has grown massively. Developed in Jamaica, reggae evolved from the genres rocksteady and ska, it is more intricate than ska but faster than rocksteady. A combination of the two genres, reggae has a more compounded style of music with much more depth. No one is quite sure where the reggae sound came from but there are many theories about its origin.

Let us first look at Derrick Morgan's theory which states that people didn't like the slowness of the rocksteady genre so he tried a different version of Fat Man, a more soulful beat. Due to this the producer Bunny Lee; created a tempo for the song using the organ and the rhythm guitar. The beat sounded like it was reggae- reggae- reggae just like a drum would go boom- boom- boom. Bunny Lee started using the word to define the sound and soon after other musicians followed.

Toots Hibbert had a different theory. He stated that while playing around one morning with his friends he said "let's do the reggae". This was a word he claimed that just popped into his mind unconsciously and slipped out of his mouth. After that they just started singing, "do the reggae, do the reggae" and created a beat which was not odd since most beats formulated in those times depended mainly on impulse and sudden realistic inspirations. He explained that people later told them that they gave the sound its name as no one really had a standard name for the rocksteady/ ska off-spring.

It was also said that Bob Marley told of the word reggae being derived from a Spanish term, referring to the King's music. Later, reggae gospel singers also stated it was derived from the Latin word regi, which means to the king. Even though the issue of who founded reggae has not been settled, one thing we are sure of is that there are many great contributors; we thank them all. Great thanks go to Toots and The Maytals, Derrick Morgan, John Holt, Alton Ellis, Marcia Griffiths, Yellow Man and all of the other reggae greats. We also want to specially recognize Bob Marley for his contribution of making reggae international and Jimmy Cliff for taking reggae to the cinemas.

Rastafarians play a noteworthy part in reggae, with their drumming and their strong sense of African styles being present in recordings of various reggae singles and albums. It was through them the influence of reggae, being related to the ancestors and mother Africa which is mostly referred to as 'The Motherland", took form. This is one of the reasons we see most reggae singers sporting dread locks as most moved to take on the Rastafarian religion, but not all.

Others who deserve recognition in the development of reggae include: Clancy Eccles, Lee 'Scratch' Perry, Larry Marshall, Johnny Nash, Millie Small, Chris Blackwell (who founded Island Records in the 1960s in Jamaica), The Wailers which consisted of Bob Marley, Peter Tosh and Bunny Wailer, among other great reggae contributors.

1972 was a good year for reggae as it was number one on the US Billboard's Top 100 chart in both months of September and November. The American rock band, Three Dog Night's was at number one in September with their reggae version The Maytones', "Black and White" and Johnny Nash, a Jamaican reggae artist, was at number one for four consecutive weeks in November with his single "I Can See Clearly Now", which was famously covered by Jimmy Cliff in 1993 for the movie Cool Running's. A lot of us can relate to singing this song aloud at some time or another; whether young or old. It was even a lead sound track in the well-known 1998 animated movie, "ANTZ" and countless others.

In the 80's reggae started to transform, giving birth to what we call dancehall music which is now dominant on its own. At the same time, reggae-pop also surfaced, flourishing throughout that period. It's classified under reggae fusion which consists of a mixture of two or more of these (with reggae being the dominant style); reggae, ska, lovers rock, pop, rhythm and blues, rock and contemporary R&B. Dominant sounds were from instruments such as bass, drums, guitars, organs, brass, synthesizers, samplers and drum machines. In this era artists like Ziggy Marley, Shaggy, Shabba, Maxi Priest and others came on to add something more to reggae. This younger generation was making reggae their own. Reggae fusion was dominant straight into the mid-90s where we saw artists like Buju Banton, Bounty Killer, Beenie Man, Sean Paul, Diana King and others rising to give their contribution to the reggae music industry. For some, this was the best time for reggae and for others the climax was from the late-60s and throughout the 70s.

Reggae took a turn in Jamaica in the late-90s going into the 21st century. Musicians began to move away from dancehall and toward a more technical and up-tempo sound. Some would say that this evolution was forgetting the true meaning of reggae music leading to a dark period in the genre but it didn't die. Some true reggae producers will tell you that reggae is no longer the same because the land of its birth seems to have turned its back on it. Some of what they now call reggae in today's music industry isn't really reggae. What began as a simple distraction in the late-90s is now a trend, where music for some is no longer made from real instruments and time well spent with a band, but is instead created using computers and other electronic tools which allows for faster music production. Let's think of a nice Jamaican ackee and salt-fish breakfast and how great the taste is. In order to make the ackee and salt-fish dish you must soak and boil the salt out of the fish, scald or boil your ackees, prepare your seasonings and follow the necessary steps for a perfect outcome. Now what would happen if you should skip boiling that salt of the fish? It would almost be the same on the surface, it might smell the same but it would definitely not taste the same-some would say it lacks the authentic flavor. That is how some modern reggae music comes across to dedicated reggae fans, all because some composers want the easier way out.

Some older artists and some dedicated new reggae artists still stick to their original vibrant bands to create their sound, fulfilling the meaning and path of a true reggae vibe. For instance, in 1998, Groundation, a white reggae band who uses real instruments to create their sounds, collaborated with and captured the hearts of great legends like Pablo Moses, Ashanti Roy (the Congos) and Winston Jarrett. Reggae is loved by many around the world and even though it now seems a little watered down in Jamaica, the fact still remains that it was originated by Jamaicans in Jamaica.

America and Europe are now the foster homes of reggae; that is where the strength of reggae now lies. Yes, we still have note-worthy people in Jamaica who are dedicated to the cause and who are great ambassadors of reggae but let us face the facts; Europe and America have adapted quite well to building authentic reggae music hands. There are Jamaican artists living in Jamaica who love and perform reggae music exclusively; they acknowledge the fact that there are currently only a handful of local producers who are creating original reggae beats. What is commonly being used in reggae right now are computer composed beats which just don't give you the same feeling, no matter how good it sounds. One artist, who prefers not to be named, told me that in order to get the sound he really needs, he has connected to someone in Europe who creates reggae beats he feels are much better than those of the composers he is associated with in his own country of Jamaica. Otherwise, he would have to take his band to the studio which is by far a much greater expense. He states that there are some great composers in Jamaica but he just hasn't had the opportunity to work with them and that the "guys in Europe", even though they integrate the computers with their live bands to create beats, are more professionally trained to monitor the sounds and effects thus, they don't come off so artificial and it's easier to integrate your lyrics. He also states that Jamaicans are more dedicated to creating dancehall beats and most of these beats come out a whole lot better than anything else they try but most end up sounding identical because the composers stick to a popular trend. They compete to be the one to make the next hot rhythm to dominate the airwaves and seem to forget the joy of motivational music. I couldn't help but wonder if the cause of this was due to the fact most composers are on the younger side of life and maybe they feel reggae has done its time. Then I realized that this couldn't be the reason since a lot of international reggae composers are fairly young people.

Take a look at some of the people who will be featured in this book and also take a look at the billboard reggae charts, where Jamaicans artists are often absent and no, it's not bashing, instead, it's acknowledging the fact that reggae has changed over the years. These artists, who are dominating the reggae charts; love Jamaica and they love reggae, thus, they made the choice of being reggae artists. How can Jamaica be the mother of something they no longer nurture? No need to fool ourselves; our reggae baby grew up and migrated. I believe that Jamaica needs to support their reggae industry a lot more. Still, I am proud of these artists from around the world who didn't allow the fact that they are not Jamaicans to stop them from conquering something they love. They took the challenge, going into a genre they appreciate, doing something different from those around them and investing in it to rise above the waters and grow.

After saying all of that, I want to look at the positive side of Jamaica and reggae. No matter how the other parts of the world seem to be dominating, people still prefer to see Jamaicans do reggae. Even though we don't know for sure who started it, we sure know where it started so we need to nurture it. It's not about who makes the next best rhythm at all times but sometimes it's about who makes the next rhythm that will be played for generations to come. We also need to remember that reggae holds no grudge; reggae focuses on music for relaxation, justice and uplifting the spirit; so I would suggest young artists cut back on being too caught up in the guns, crimes and riches; instead, work on creating something everyone can relate to. It all begins with the younger generation. Will we rise to regain our roots or will we leave it up to others to dominate? I want to commend Chronixx and Etana, two of the young Jamaican reggae artists right now and some of those awesome young reggae bands we see appearing on the prominent TVJ program Layers Of Souls. I also commend artists like Jah Cure, Sizzla, Protoje, Queen Ifrica, all of the young Marleys, Etana, and other artists who have made reggae their own.

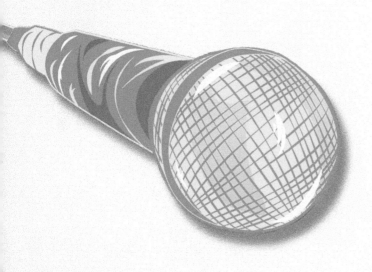

Conkarah

Reggae Artist

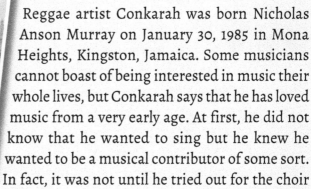

Reggae artist Conkarah was born Nicholas Anson Murray on January 30, 1985 in Mona Heights, Kingston, Jamaica. Some musicians cannot boast of being interested in music their whole lives, but Conkarah says that he has loved music from a very early age. At first, he did not know that he wanted to sing but he knew he wanted to be a musical contributor of some sort. In fact, it was not until he tried out for the choir at his university that he discovered his voice. From that moment on, singing became his passion and his journey has been an incredible one.

Conkarah was raised in a two-parent household along with one younger sister. His parents were supportive, excellent role models, and he even goes on to say that they were "cool." How many children really think their parents are cool? His parents have always been his biggest supporters, along with his sisters, with whom he has maintained a very close relationship through the years.

Having been raised in such a warm home, it stands to reason that his childhood should have been quite the enjoyable one. Indeed, Conkarah describes his growing up as fun and relatively normal. He remembers riding his bike through the community and playing football (or as the Americans say, soccer)-with his friends. In fact, football continues to be his favourite hobby to this day.

You would think that loving something as rugged as football would make him just as rugged a person, but he is the exact opposite. Conkarah is a very charitable person who believes in happiness and in making people happy. "[Happiness] just spreads good vibes so that in itself is just a huge inspiration for me," he says. He is also inspired by people who follow their dreams and stand up for what they believe in. The people who inspire him the most are those he has met in his day-to-day life and, most importantly, his family. He is not married but would like to be as he regards family highly; he has been blessed with good health, a good education, and an open mind—a mind that turns the bad things in life into something hopeful. "There are many things that rub me the wrong way, but I've learned to be understanding and to realize that there is a reason for everything," says Conkarah. He tries not to have regrets about his career or anything for that matter and whenever he makes a mistake, he learns from it and moves on.

That kind of attitude is a very fortunate one to possess, especially when one is in the music business which can be a very trying experience. Conkarah has had to overcome his fair share of challenges as does every musician and more specifically, he had to learn to believe in himself and trust his own decisions. However, despite whatever hardships he has had to face in his career, Conkarah continues to love music and is motivated by what his music has the potential to do. He wants to make a positive impact on the world through his music which he has heard others term "sunshine reggae," though he describes it as "a 'likkle' reggae music infused into different genres." This is what the music industry calls reggae fusion.

Music and career aside, there are many other things that Conkarah enjoys. We already know that he loves football but he also has a passion for cinematography. In fact, he admits that if he did not have a career in music, he would have liked to have had one in cinematography which is very fascinating. Conkarah's favourite fruits are grapes, which he perhaps likes to eat while reading his favourite book 'The Alchemist' by Paulo Coelho and jerking chicken. However, his absolute favourite food is coconut. "I love coconuts above everything though. When I drink one of those and eat the jelly, I feel as though I've de-aged about two years." So are coconuts the secret to a prosperous musical career?

Conkarah is a true-spirited musician, not only does he sing, but he also plays the guitar and piano. He is very selective of the kinds of music he listens to and his preference rings of his passion for music he only enjoys songs comprising of lyrics that speak to him. He respects musicians who are true to their lyrics and in a sense practice what they preach. He is not one to choose a favourite song, whether it be his own or someone else's and Conkarah's reason for this is simple as he states, "each song has its own special place in my heart."

Nevertheless, he doesn't need a favourite song to love music or deliver it to his fans. He revels in the gift he has been given and is so thankful that he has the opportunity to perform the music he loves in front of thousands of people. From the moment he became a part of the music industry, he has done things he never would have dreamed of before, such as performing for over 20,000 people at Sunfest and flying to Europe to perform. Conkarah has been blessed with an extraordinary opportunity to follow his dreams and share his music with the world; he can only hope that he will continue to inspire others with his passion.

Kym

Reggae-Dancehall-R&B Artist

Kym Monique Hamilton was born in Kingston, Jamaica on December 5, 1990. She grew up in Portmore, St. Catherine, which is where she currently resides when not traveling. She is the youngest of the family with three sisters and four brothers and felt that she was pampered growing up by her siblings and mother. Living with just her mother, she was everything to Kym and still is. They have a very good relationship and they talk about everything. Even though her dad was not there, he maintained the household and made sure the family was cared for.

Other than her mother, Kym is very close with her big sister. As a child she was inspired by her mother because she hardly ever showed signs of giving up when a lot of women might have. She did what she could for her family without breaking down. As Kym grew up, she remembers hearing her big sister sing every single day. Kym wanted to do everything her sister did, so she started listening to music and found inspiration in the voices of Tanya Stephens and Lady Saw. She wanted to reach the audience they reached so she started singing at school and entering competitions just to make sure that she was heard. Now her nephew is following in her footsteps by joining the school choir, entering school festivals, and he has been doing a little song writing as well.

Both good and bad things have happened to Kym in the short time she has been in the music business, but she has no regrets. Instead, she believes everything, whether good or bad, happens for a reason and that without mistakes there would be no lessons learned. One good thing that has happened in her career was being nominated for an award from the British Reggae Industry and World Reggae Music alongside Queen Ifrica and Tanya Stephens. Even though she did not win, she felt like a winner because those two ladies are her heroes, and to be nominated with them was a truly win for her. In the future, Kym hopes to win a few Grammys so she keeps hard at work. Kym's main challenge is

regaining her fans; unfortunately, she lost them due to circum-stances a few years ago. Anyway, since she believes everything happens for a reason, with the help of God she is determined and believes she will regain them; she has no intention of ever giving up.

As an advocate of women's rights, she hates that female artists, especially in Jamaica, are not treated fairly. She feels that women have to work thrice as hard but are still not appreciated. She would love to change that, but knows that only God can change the mindset of other people. However, she enjoys that her career allows her meet new people and to explore new places. Kym does not remember the first time she fell in love with music, but she has been singing for over seven years. She is able to sing from her life experiences, from things happening in her community and things happening in the world. She is driven by love, her family, and most of all, the people that say she will never make it.

Her favourite music is reggae/dancehall, which is the type of music she performs. Reggae and dancehall are the entrance to the heart and soul of all Jamaicans and their music is loved worldwide. Kym also sings R&B, but reggae is her rhythm. She is inspired by all of the female artists holding their own in the music business, especially Queen Ifrica. Her favourite song that she has written is, "Got to Go Right Now," which was produced by Payday Music Group, but she loves to perform "Come Round a Mi Yard" (a remix of a song by Movado). While she does not play an instrument right now, she hopes to play the guitar one day.

Kym is not married and does not have any kids but she would love to have some on day. She also hopes that someone will "pop the question" to her one day. Honesty, good manners, respect, and most of all a friendly attitude are valued by her. She also believes that chil-dren are the future and that they should be cherished and groomed for their future. She hates to see children suffer, so anything that she can do, no matter how small it is, she will do to help them.

When asked what she is most thankful for, her answer was her family, who along with being her biggest supporters, motivate her to do her best. In fact, they tell it as they see it. She thanks God every day for the gift He gave her, because her music is her therapy when things get rough. She is still trying to find out who she is but music allows her to be whoever she wants to be; singing brings out the different characters within her.

Her hobbies include hairdressing, designing clothes and of course singing. Topping that off, she has a passion for art, yes, she loves to draw and if she was not a reggae singer, she would be doing art. Her favourite author is Dr. Seuss; in addition, she loves to read the Holy Bible because from it keeps her be grounded. Her favourite dish is brown stewed chicken with boiled dumplings, yams and green bananas.

CEE-GEE

Dancehall-Reggae Artist

Port Antonio, Jamaica, has contributed its share of talent to the reggae world and with the birth of Cheston Grosset, also known as Cee Gee, Port Antonio provided reggae with another gem. A lover of all music, Cee Gee is a dancehall artist with a lyrical flow that moves the people as much as the riddim. The only musician in his family, Mr. Grosset is no stranger to struggle. Son of single mother, the dancehall musician often found strength in his late grandmother whose memory he cherishes dearly. "I have had a lot of good child-hood memories but if I had to choose one, I would say times spent with my now deceased grandmother. Grandma imparted a great deal of knowledge to me and I'm so grateful to have had her in my life; If I had to choose one of my many influences, it would be her," said Grosset. Using the lessons that his grandmother has given him along with the inspiration from his son Jhae, his mother, and the rest of his family (a sister and two brothers) plus friends, "Di Lyrical Martian"

consistently delivers music of substance and constantly works towards perfection. "I need to be the best I can be so my son has an exemplary figure to look up to."

"My professional goals are limitless, beyond the sky," Cee Gee goes on to say. It doesn't take long to realize that Cheston Grosset is more than a musician. He is a father and a role model inside and outside the music industry. "I love music and I'm grateful for every chance I get to do it. Although there are many things in the music industry I don't like, the only step I think I can take to change anything is to do what's right and lead by example so the ones looking up to me will only see me and my work in a positive light," states the dedicated artist. Cee Gee's work does not stop at music; he also dedicates himself to those in need. "I'm inspired to do charitable work just by knowing that every act of kindness will be rewarded with blessing from the most high. I myself have benefitted from charity so I have no problem doing charitable deeds," he told LBRM. Cee Gee is a lover of mangoes and ripe bananas which is not a surprise as Portland is known for its bountiful cultivation of bananas which the artist might have fallen in love with from a young age. With God as his guide, he intends to make the lives of his family and friends just as sweet as his favourite fruits: "My personal goal is to elevate my family and friends to a level of comfort, helping them to fulfill their dreams and aspirations."

With style, talent and dedication, it comes as no surprise that music has taken Cee Gee as far as Africa and with songs such as Stayin Alive and Sittn Sittn, Cee Gee has proven himself a real deal reggae artist, holding his own on riddims with the likes of Beenie Man. Cee Gee creates the music he grew up on, the music he loves most of all and his love for music has inspired him to learn to play keyboard: "I do not play instruments but I recently bought a Keystation Mini 32, so the next time I'm asked the question if I play any particular instrument, the answer will probably be yes," the artist shared.

Currently music, family and friends are Cee Gee's only loves; although he has known the pain of heartbreak, love may be on the horizon for the reggae performer: "Yes I have been in love. Maybe I am right now," he states. His status as a bachelor may be a mystery. There is no questioning Cee Gee's humility and perseverance. "I've been faced with a lot of challenges but I'm just like everyone else. We were not promised an easy path to success so I just jump one hurdle at a time." Constantly, conditioning his heart and mind, Cee Gee is poised to become reggae's next big star and with only eight years in professional music, the future of Mr. Cheston Grosset would appear to be nothing short of promising.

ESCO

Dancehall Producer Reggae Artist

Few artists dare erase the lines that separate the genres; Esco is not one of those artists. Matthew Thompson was born, on August 16th at St Joseph's Hospital in Kingston, Jamaica. Esco is a rarity of sorts. That is if you call blending hip–hop, pop, reggae and dancehall to create one seamless sound a strange thing. Esco grew up in the Kingston 6 Area with his mother, four brothers and sister. Music inspired this Caribbean fusion artist at the age of eight, listening to reggae and dancehall music from the likes of Buju Banton, Bounty Killer and Sean Paul. Mr. Thompson is a keyboardist as well as a vocalist and is one of four musicians in his family; Esco's two brothers, his father and step mother are all musicians.

As stereotypes go, Esco is far from your typical musician, in fact he tries his best to stay away from the systematic and rigid, to present music that is not one particular sound but many. Make no mistake, Esco is a true island artist but he can be heard bringing reggae vibes to mainstream rap and hip-hop instrumentals. Songs like "Gentle", "Di Show is Over" and "Root of all Evil" all illustrate Esco's ability to fuse genres. Driven by his mother's inspiration and the support of his girlfriend, Esco keeps his eyes on the prize, success being a big motivator for the father of one. Since his father Errol Thompson was a disc jockey and married to Marcia Griffiths, Esco grew up very close to music; it was not unusual for this side of Esco's family to travel. The support that Esco 'Da Shocker' received as a boy is a prime example of what a supportive and encouraging household can do for children. Esco's mother raised him in a middle class home, where manners and a strong character were instilled in him at an early age.

Presently, he resides in Cherry Gardens, Jamaica, where he fondly reflects on his accomplishments, being a father is his proudest, his good memories of time spent with friends, winning awards and passing his CXC (Caribbean Examination Council) subjects. When Matthew Thompson isn't in the studio or on the stage he enjoys watching sports, particularly watching basketball. If not for his successful music career, Esco would have taken his chances in the NBA. Esco's favourite book, Conversations with God by Neale Walsch. Similar to his approach in music, Esco is a fan of an array of foods and is not a man to favor one dish over another. Of his relations, Esco is closest to his mother and siblings and though he is not yet married, he is currently in love and hopes to one day to be a husband who values honesty and respect.

Esco is truly blessed to have health and happiness and neither heartbreak nor hurdle could prevent this reggae fusion artist from reaching his dreams. In fact, Esco has returned to the music business after once being a part of a prominent group that decided to call it quits. He believes that life is a journey of choices and that destiny is training towards the greater good; for this reason, Esco is inspired to give to charity in an attempt to uplift children in need. By reaching his goal of becoming a U.S. millionaire, Mr. Thompson hopes to be able to evoke the change he wishes to see.

As his music suggests, Esco is an open minded man and though he has had to overcome classist prejudice to become the musician he is today, music has afforded Esco the opportunity to work by his own initiative; nevertheless, there are aspects of the music industry that Esco is not particularly fond of, specifically, the lawlessness and lack of principles within the industry. The industry may not be perfect but it has created a platform for Esco's unique brand of music. It can be said with confidence that the Esco show is far from over.

Cali P

Reggae Artist

If you are exposed to music from the first day you drew breath, chances are, music will always have a special place in your heart. Such is the case with Zurich, Switzerland born Pierre Nanon, also known as Cali P. Born February 17th, 1985, his father a fellow musician introduced Pierre to music during infancy, with the pulsating rhythms of Gwo Ka. The vocalist/drummer has not strayed from the course. "I was just born into music. From when I was a baby laying on the ground I lay beside the materials that my father had to build drums. Constantly we listened to drum music GwoKa and reggae and early dancehall: black music, soul, African music, all together. Music had all my interest when I grew up. So much that when I had to decide for a job it could have only been

15

music." As a boy, splitting his time between Switzerland and Pointe a Pitre Gaudeloupe, Cali P travelled frequently; his fondest memories are attending concert sound checks, watching the artists set up for shows, performing with his father, and creating choreography with his sister with whom he is extremely close.

In music and in life, Pierre's mother and been consummate parents and role models. "I loved my childhood. I grew up with my two parents. I was free to choose any instruments, sports, livity, I say livity because my papa is a Rasta but I was never forced to be the same. My parents just teach me righteousness and manners... my parents are sometimes so far yet still so close. My mother is simply my greatest love. I might live in Jamaica and she in Switzerland, and we might not talk everyday but we know exactly what we mean to each other. My mommy was always a good teacher to me, always keep me positive and is very supportive in whatever I want to do or let's say nearly whatever I do; my dad, same thing, one of my idols. He is the most natural person I know, doesn't take no talk from Babylon. He was never into no form of brainwash system, as my dad himself grow in a very special way; real sufferer that has achieved great things. I have nothing but endless love for him because he is always there for me. I don't know a handful of people who can say that about their father. He is just great and has made me love my culture and traditions very much. He grows me up in a place that is not set for Rasta and still has achieved to keep me on a good way without forcing it on me. I think that's really what makes me be me at the end of the day."

It would appear as if Cali P could not fight the Rasta vibrations as he too wears the crown, producing conscious music similar to that of Dennis Brown, Bob Marley, Buju Banton, Sizzla Kalonji, Bounty Killer, Feta Kuti, Michael Jackson and the Dub-step duo Sly and Robbie who have all influenced this Reggae artist to perform with the experience in mind, creating a groove that carries a message. Cali P has performed professionally since the age of 13 and since that time has evolved as an artist, incorporating various sounds to his brand of music. "My music has no limits. If I feel to sing on a dancehall riddim

I do that just as feeling a roots riddim and go into a deep meditation... That's me, a modern roots youth."

A perfect example of Cali P's free flowing creativity is 'Dreadful', a track with a hip hop sound underlying a roots message. It is this freedom in music that Cali P enjoys most and he intends to take this sound around the world; he wishes to influence others positively as he has been influenced, overcoming the negative aspects of the music industry. "I don't like when people feel like they alone can make music business and try everything to fight out others because they afraid to lose position and things like that. The world never has enough of music and creativity so there is space for all of us, really all, and that's how we should move. Reggae/dancehall could be the strongest music worldwide, only if all unite and know the strength of each other... I want to be able to produce music, release music with a good team and tour the world...I am a perfectionist when it comes to my music. I love when it grooves, that's perfection there, groove. Playing music like it's a language. I love to involve the crowd into the show. And I perform reggae, dancehall, hip hop and R&B."

One of the most impactful experiences during Pierre Nanon's extensive travelling has been his trips to Africa which gave him purpose in life: "Before I ever traveled to Jamaica I had traveled Africa four times. In that time I learned my mission in life. And there comes a lot of charitable works. I see myself as a person that has a lot of different missions in different countries. But everything comes to Africa if you understand what I mean. That's the point of centralization, my future. Right now I am not in the position to spend on certain projects that I would like but I am building towards that. And I always do the best to open doors for people." Until his dreams come to fruition, Cali P enjoys Kingston, Jamaica, a place that helps him keep life in perspective, reminding him to be grateful for life and all his blessings. Cali P states "Life itself is the greatest. Opening the eyes in the morning is something I never take for granted because sometimes you get some news of people that leave you and you have never imagined that would happen for a second so I am thankful I can see, feel, hear, smell all these things ... It is true that musicians tend to get good treatment. I always say I get royal treatment because I am a King. And that is how I live, royal. When I am outside in the streets I bless up the people them and I give thanks for them. Maybe they don't even know sometimes."

Every kingdom must rightfully have a King as well as a Queen and though Cali P has never been heartbroken, the separation of his parents at age 12 has left him skeptical about marriage. "I have one daughter. Seeing how my life has been going so far I am disappointed with marriage. My parents were married and they are not anymore. People are fine with each other for years UNTIL they get married. I really don't know about marriage for now but I know there is only one person I can get married to in my life." Cali P ranks the separation of his parents as one of his most difficult emotional hardships along with the loss of his grandfather. Five siblings have come as a result of his parent's separation. Though he isn't rushing to make any vows, it hasn't stopped this reggae artist from knowing the warmth of love. Disappointment is only one of the obstacles Cali P has had to overcome in life but through it all he relies on his faith and mother earth to provide. "I had to be able to live and communicate anywhere I am at in the world. The only way to do this is look beyond race, faith, and culture, beyond even what is right to me and what is right to others. I had to learn to live life to the fullest. Now I am there, I know where I am from and where I am going so I am able to communicate with anyone in this world without feeling like I am out of this world or they are. Today I know we are all one... Jah the almighty give me strength every day to attack again and again... Mama Earth gives me water to function and do all I do."

A man of faith, family, love and unity, Cali P lives without regret knowing that each test, each moment of laughter, and each tear is a part of the growing process of life. The vocalist enjoys cooking and eating ackee as well as an array of fruits from all over the world (each independently, never mixed). Cali P also enjoys playing basketball (his other dream job would be the NBA). Though his career as a musician has taken most of his time, he still remains close to his friends all over the globe. Cali P is driven by the joy of creativity and hopes that one day in old age he will have a marvelous story to tell of his accomplishments. Until that time, the reggae artist keeps life in perspective, gives Jah the praise, and keeps the fire burning.

Damas

Producer-Reggae Artist

Damas was born Christopher Williams on a wonderful December day of the 20th century in Kingston, Jamaica in the area of Arnette Garden. Christopher describes his early childhood as average. Music, though, has been a part of his life and continues to be his passion and driving force.

Christopher grew up in a single parent household and to this day he maintains a relationship with his mother, however, it cannot be said that it is a particularly close one. Despite not having a close relationship with anyone in his family, he does feel particularly intimate with God and his religion. Religion has been an inspiration to him from an early age and it continues to motivate him to create music and to do charitable works.

20

Furthermore, Christopher finds inspiration in Mother Teresa, Malcolm X, Martin Luther King, and more profoundly, in life itself. He is very thankful for the life he is able to live and because of it and the figures mentioned above, he is driven to give back to those who are less fortunate and to move others with his uplifting music.

Although his career has not provided much in the way of freedom or things of that sort, Christopher takes comfort in the fact that his music is able to teach and unite people all over the world despite any boundaries of nationality. His music is "cool and collected" and keeps people balanced with its steady vibe. Since his professional debut in 2006, Christopher has overcome many obstacles both musically and personally. He has had to surpass stereotypes, stigmatism, as well as his own fears and doubts.

Nevertheless, Christopher has become a musical success. He is most proud of his single "Rasta Universal Love" and the opportunity he had to go on tour in Europe. His favourite song written by him to date is "Rise Over" but his favourite song to perform is "One Chance." Christopher is grateful for everything he has accomplished and he owes it all to his own hard work and determination. Throughout any hardships he has had to face, Christopher himself has been his biggest supporter, which is very inspirational not only to fellow musicians, but to anyone who strives to follow a dream that seems impossible to grasp. He is a wonderful example of what can happen when one doesn't let opposition get in the way of what he or she wants.

Christopher still has many things he wishes to accomplish, such as finding a way to make his record label more successful, expand into the multimedia world, and to help others find the career of their dreams. He even hopes to one day get married and have children. Judging by what he has accomplished so far in his life as a result of his own willpower, there can be no doubt he will succeed in anything he puts his mind to.

Denyque

Pop-R&B-Dancehall Reggae Artist

A great series, good plot and cars can get this girl going. From being "daddy's little girl" to becoming an independent woman who is aware and secure in her femininity, the growth has definitely been a true transformation for her. She can be your "Supergirl" once you become "Hooked on Me"; all these songs have helped this young lady transition from academia to becoming a star. Born in the parish of St. James, Jamaica, celebrating her birthday on February 21st and raised between the parishes of Westmoreland and Manchester; enter stage left: Denyque Dontre Welds. With an introduction such as this, of course she must be a shining star.

Her creativity stems from characters that have inspired her from literature and film which she has infused into her music. Dr. Seuss and Disney characters are big on her list. Her music draws inspiration from R&B, reggae, dancehall and pop thus creating an eclectic sound and feel to her songs. Any fan of hers may have come to realize that R&B is her favourite genre of music. Her influences in this genre from as far back as The Spinners to present-day art-ists like- Beyoncé. Her musical path began with the realization that she had a talent that had to be shared with the world. Not only for her fans to hear her unique voice, but also in remaining true to herself.

She was raised by her mother and father and is the youngest of her siblings; discipline, independence and ambition were drilled into her psyche over the years from her father. All which have been a standard and benchmark which she has strived for both person-ally and professionally. Denyque's biggest support comes from her family especially in the form of her nieces and nephews, she truly values this. Not only does she appreciate the support from her family but is also thankful for her management team (her powerhouse) behind her music.

Being a female in a male dominated profession can be quite taxing but Denyque handles it with a cool head. Having convinced the alpha male in her life, her father, no doubt navigating this busi-ness will be less of a challenge. With her future goals and ambitions formulated she takes the next step in becoming a brand. Coming from a country girl that was raised by parents that instilled positive principles with education as the foundation, Denyque has found a niche for herself. Being competitive by nature compels her to succeed whether she'd been an architectural engineer, criminal lawyer or psychologist. Though she may be the only musician in her family, she gained grounds by singing from an early age and extending her musical repertoire by playing basic piano. The music has transformed this little country girl into a corporate woman who now resides in Kingston, the mecca of dancehall and reggae.

"The lack of structure and unity, reggae and dancehall belongs to us and the sooner we recognize this and work towards a more unified brand to drive us internationally we would have already done something spectacular", notes Denyque. Although the unity may be lacking, she does not allow this to affect her; there is a work hard, play hard with no regrets mentality for this young lady. Denyque is thankful for a healthy body and soul and as the master of her destiny she pushes forward to accomplish her goals. She sees none of her accomplishments as more than the other for they all have contributed to the woman she is today: Denyque. The responsibility of being a celebrity is taken with a gravity and seriousness and she uses this platform to inspire and impact her peers and fans.

Her love for the arts has drawn her particularly to students who are labeled as "slow learners". For example, there are students that have to process information in a visual way and therefore, the traditional way of teaching has done nothing for them. Her hope is that more schools will implement teaching aids that will reach these students and as such working with these children is part of her outreach effort.

An Harry Potter aficionado who not only feeds on this series but also upon star apples, guineps, lychee and strawberries along with a good plate of pasta or curried shrimp. Her hobbies are wide and varied, ranging from books and movies to cars. Denyque may not have any children at the moment but a husband and children are a part of her life's dream. As for Denyque the star, look out world for there is more to come from this budding world-class entrepreneur.

Dax Lion

Roots-Reggae Artist

"A friend once told me the reason [I became a musician] and I can't explain it. Music is in my blood; maybe that's the explanation."

Perhaps Dax Lion really does have musical blood in his veins. However, it takes more than that to make it to the big time. It takes drive, inspiration, and dedication to make a song in the heart something real. So what influenced Dax to become a musician? What made him land in a territory far different and unexpected from the place he began?

Dax Lion grew up in a two-parent household in Maryland, St. Andrew in Jamaica (although he was born in Kingston and currently resides in the United States) along with his brother and sister. His father sells coconuts and does tire repairs, and his mother works for airlines, mostly, but is an artist on the side, who makes jewelry and other accessories. Dax's childhood was very active and he was heavily involved in sports. His father made sure he was active and wanted his son to play tennis, specifically. All of his young life was occupied by the sport. Many people don't know this about Dax, but he once represented Jamaica worldwide in tennis for years. "I took it to heart and believed that I was going to be the best tennis player on earth at the time." So what changed?

Well, for starters, high school happened. They say high school is where passions are created and dreams are realized and for Dax high school was where he first discovered his passion for music. "We used to gather as friends and someone would be doing a beat on the table and we would all try and sing like another artist and sing over songs that were popular. I remember this clearly. This was where my interest first began."

It was also during these early years of discovery that Dax encountered two men that would become prime sources of inspiration for him: Michael Jackson and Bob Marley. These men unlocked a door for him and showed him what it was like to have music in your soul. Dax remembers watching Michael Jackson's 30th Anniversary Concert on tv and Bob Marley's Live Performance DVDs and to this day their performances are stuck in his mind. These men taught Dax what it meant to be a musician.

Not long after his eyes were opened to the world of music did Dax receive his first big break and his first chance to become a serious musician. After watching a tape of Dax singing, Kimani Robinson, the owner of Reggae Entertainment Television (RETV) at the time, invited Dax to meet with various artists and producers in the industry. Ever since then, Dax has been working on his craft and making a name for himself as a reggae artist.

Of course, nothing is without its challenges and that includes pursuing a career in the music industry, which has its fair share of competitors and naysayers. But sometimes it's best to look at these challenges as stepping stones of sorts—necessary obstacles along the path that in the end make the experience and the result that much more rewarding. For example, Dax used to have to sleep outside the studios in Jamaica waiting for a chance to record. Sometimes, he didn't even get his chance, which meant he spent all that time get-

ting sunburned for no reason. But the challenges he has had to face just made him more determined to reach his goals. "I have felt hurt in my heart before; I think every-one in this world has, as well. It's just called 'Life'—things happen, but it toughened me up and made me the person I am today as a musician. My work ethic is constant—I always want to make music and create and write. It's a life mission to me that is almost divine in a sense."

But despite these challenges, Dax is proud of everything he has accomplished thus far in his career. Music has opened doors for him and allowed him to see places he would never have seen and meet people he never would have met in any other circumstances. His music means everything to him. Yes, he might love to cook his famous "Dax Lion Bean Stew," but music is his sustenance, as well as his hobby and his life. And while he does wish he could play more instruments like his cousin Andy Vernon (Dax plays only the acoustic guitar), he is very thankful for the one instrument he was blessed with at birth: his voice. "I like that I have a 'voice'. I get to speak my mind and express myself through my music. Performing is like nothing else in this world. My soul is at ease and feels satisfied in the aftermath."

Music is what drives him, especially reggae music. Dax loves all kinds of music, but reggae holds a special place in his heart, especially because he finds that it is the only genre that encompasses all other genres. He believes within reggae music one can find elements of jazz, pop, rock, R&B, etc. This is all-inclusive element of reggae is what makes it sound so good to Dax. According to him, it gives the music a certain quality that cannot be resisted.

Speaking of songs that can't be resisted, one of Dax's favourite songs to sing is his "Gwan Natty." It is a fun song that is full of good vibes and energy. "It made me smile while I was recording it and still makes me smile when I hear it." He likes to perform this song, too, but his favourite song to perform is "Gas Pon It" because not only is it one of the first songs he ever recorded, but it makes him feel closer to God. Dax wrote the song when he was deep in prayer and he feels as though it was sent to him by God. "It's really his words." In fact, Dax credits God and the Bible for most of his inspiration. For him, God is his biggest supporter along with his family and friends.

A support group is essential for a musician and Dax's group is what helps him get through every obstacle he faces. "I am driven by my family. My mother and father are my rocks, my teachers and leaders." But Dax is not only inspired the people themselves, he is inspired by the life they gave him and raised him in. "I am driven in the pursuit of happiness, by the inequalities of the world, and the hopes of making it better. I am driven by people that I come in contact with daily. Basically, I am driven just by the experience of the life I am having now and by the teachings from great leaders and the Bible. I want to be a positive impact in this world. I don't want to live life for myself; I want to live it with and for others." Life, family, and God are what move Dax to write songs of passion and love, songs that can speak to and inspire people all over the world. These people help make that song in his heart real. Musical blood or not, one thing is for sure: Dax Lion is a reggae artist with an unwavering love for the music he makes and he couldn't imagine doing anything else with his life.

Bay-C

Producer-Reggae Dancehall Artist

TOK is one of the biggest dancehall groups in and outside of Jamaica. With their amazing beats and catchy lyrics who could resist the infectious vibe of their music and so I took the time out to get to know one particular member a bit more: intro Roshaun Clarke, better known as Bay-C. He was born in London, United Kingdom on the 3rd of August 1977. He may have been born in the United Kingdom but he is a true Jamaican having grown up in Hellshire. His experiences are truly unique having seen both sides of the fence in the Jamaican socio-economic culture;

uptown and downtown, poverty and the circumstances that surround it. They may be in the same country, but they may as well have been in two different worlds.

Musicians may not be plentiful in his family, but he received the passion for music from his dad. His father loved music but was not able follow his passion because of responsibilities to his family. It is this love for music that was passed to him through his father. At the age of ten he was given the serendipitous gift of a piano which further cemented his interest in music. An ardent entrepreneur,

Bay-C constantly pushes himself to pursue his interests and accomplish his many goals. He is currently pursuing his Bachelors in law- which he admits if not for music he would already have been a lawyer, and is the owner of a record label (Bombrush Records), and he is also part owner of a digital content distribution company called Listen MI Caribbean Limited. Roshaun is determined to live his life to the fullest. He sums it up perfectly, "My goal is to be a professional lawyer specializing in IP, and at the same time release innovative products such as Listen MI News and the Blue Mountain Music Festival." More than a musician he is resolute in conquering the business world.

Would Superman have reached his fullest potential without his great love, Lois Lane, at his side? I think not. Such it is with Roshaun Clarke, who has his wife and children by his side, along with his mother, as his biggest supporters. Growing up in a household with his parents and two brothers (David and Daniel) he reminisces fondly on childhood memories where attending music events such as Sunsplash and Ring Road, with his family are vivid. Sunny days at the beach and the river or camping in the mountains are also a part of his childhood memories. Having been taught by his parents the value of human life, how to articulate himself and the importance of being courteous to all; these teach-ings remain an ingrained part of his personality. These are also qualities he values in others as well. His relationship with his parents remains strong today his father is one of his closest business advisors and his mother is his legal advisor. Grief has tainted his life with the passing of his cousin; closest confidante and as a result, he has been reluctant to open himself like that again.

To keep his body physically and spiritually healthy, he enjoys running and hiking, which allows him to achieve this balance. When in relaxation mode he can be found with his favourite book 'The Prince' by Niccolo Machiavelli or a book by his favourite author Khalil Gibran. With varying tastes in food he may be chowing down on ackee and saltfish or sushi in the same breath, however, orange and ortanigue are his favourite fruits while he loves to cook fried dumplings and mackerel. He currently resides in the Blue Mountains when he's not travelling and as such the Blue Mountain Music Festival is one of his accomplishments he is most of proud of. This festival was his vision, from the inception of the idea to the execution of the concept; to bringing it to reality. 'Solid as a Rock' by TOK and 'I'm Only Human' by Bay-C featuring. Anonymous, to date, are among his favourite songs he has written and he loves performing "The Voice" with TOK.

A risk taker at heart, he conceded that many doubted that mixing dancehall (deejaying and singjaying) with the doo-wop sound would work. After being dubbed as the 'under dogs' they had to prove their worth. It eventually worked and the group exploded big on the music scene proving hard work and perseverance works. He describes his music as 'World Music' because of its mixture of influences it pleases him when his music touches others and the effect it as on the soul. His musical influences are no doubt ground breakers in the music scene, including such artists as Bob Marley, Tracy Chapman, The Doors, and Nick Drake. True to form, playing the guitar and piano makes it evident that his favourite type of music is "acoustic, anything heavy with guitars". Being an artist and producing music professionally for 22 years can have its perks. Bay-C equates it to being more influential than a politician in the Jamaican context. He considers the ability to mobilize the people as the most important part of being a musician. Seeing the hardship and struggles that many Jamaicans go through on a daily basis moves him to be charitable in any way that he can.

As an innovator, it irks him when people in the music business constantly complain that there are no opportunities. His mantra, "I am the master of my faith, I am the Captain of my Soul," from Invictus, are words he lives by. They constantly push him and inspire him to create opportunities for himself. Improving himself, his team and his community is an important part of his journey. Although there have been decisions made by the group which may not have been the best, in hindsight, they have made him someone he is proud of being which makes him and he holds no regrets. The most important thing to be taken away from Roshaun Clarke is that he is driven by life, "Always proving the doubters wrong. Honestly...if you want me to do something, just tell me I can do it or it can't be done!"

Carol Gonzalez

Rock n Roll-Ballad Soft Rock-Reggae Artist

Who would have guessed that someone with a name as unassuming as Carol Gonzalez would leave an indelible mark in the world of reggae? Only time would tell. For a female growing up in the 60's, reggae would have been in its infancy. Carol Gonzalez grew up in Kingston, Jamaica and came into the world on August 2, 1960. She grew up in a family that surrounded her with their artistic endeavours'. Her grandfather was a saxophone player from Puerto Rico; her father was a painter and graphic artist while her mother was

the homemaker and disciplinarian. No doubt, all the music and flavour in her family inspired her, and drew her to music. Like many other interracial families during that period, her story is mixed with familial disappoints because her mother. Coming from the union of an interracial couple, Carol experienced her fair share of racism from within her own family. Despite this, her childhood was a normal one growing up with her brother and two sisters. She fondly remembers jaunts to the Cane River where her father would take her and her siblings for a bit of country fun. Her parents were a constant in her childhood and she grew up in the loving comfort of their home. Her relationship with them remained strong as she grew older. However, sadly, her father passed in 1994, but her mother is alive and remains a central part of her life.

Carol Gonzalez entered the music scene in 1978, quite by chance. Having just left high school she was working for an insurance company. By chance or by providence, a friend, Jackie Jackson, who a promoter for Lady Gigi Romp, overheard Carol singing and, asked her to sing background. Seemingly impressed with her voice, Lady Gigi Romp then asked her if she wanted to join the band. As one might say, the rest is history. One of her favourite songs she has written is "True Love". Her love for music transcends any one genre, and does not limit her to a specific genre and so besides reggae; jazz, ballads rock, and pop are some of her favourite music. She enjoys performing these genres because they allow her to practice her vocal range and soothe her spirit. She credits Quincy Jones, Stevie Wonder, Whitney Houston and Billie Holiday as musicians who have inspired her musical journey as well as Mariah Carey, Beyonce and Adele. Timeless songs such as "Nature Boy" by Nat King Cole, "Summer Time" by Sam Cooke and "Say You Love Me" by Patty Austin are favourites that she loves to perform.

She is a powerhouse whether she was on the bench or expressing her soul. Music was not her only passion. Seeing the atrocities that abound in society, it moved her to pursue a legal career and as such she served on the bench for 10 years. "The music career has been the vine in my life, I have been fortunate to have a great voice, my career as a lawyer has allowed me to travel, and music wants me to travel and I am being pulled both ways and never got to pursue both careers to the fullest way I wanted." She has since given up her job as a judge and as regretted this choice. However, she has not given up her pursuit in fighting the injustice she sees. She may not be on the bench, but she continues to fight for the powerless and voiceless. Carol is a part of Woman Inc. where she counsels women in crisis and offers legal aide. She says she is most proud of these accomplishments, along with her three number one hit songs in 1992: Second Class, Spoiled by Your Love and Personal Delivery. Her love for music does not blind her to the changes that need to be made within the music industry. She countered that, "females are not recognized unless they are providing some sort of adult exchange. There are some labels that only produce music for men." She cited that artists should not be charging people to play their music at venues; it should be free of charge.

Carol's passion is not only exhibited in her music but also extends to her family. She is married with three children. She is thankful for her children and the voice she is imbued with. Though may not have faced many challenges her supporters where many. Her greatest supporter is her daughter Danielle. She counts her relationship with her daughter and her sisters as a blessing and is especially close to them. Like any Jamaican some of Carol's favourite foods are ackee and salt fish, johnny cake, curried lobster, East Indian mango and the Parisian dish chicken cordon bleu. She has an eclectic taste in books and authors ranging from Steven King, and George Martine to, Homer and Charles Dickens; and from Lord of the Rings, Vampire Chronicles, Hit, and The Shining to Wuithering Heights. She can be found enjoying Kalooki, reading a good book, swimming, watching a movie or playing tennis. Carol is not the only musician in her family. Although she cannot play an instrument, her daughters play both the violin and piano. Honesty, integrity, loyalty, compassion and love and affection without motive are qualities that she values in an individual.

"I am motivated in my legal career by injustice, and I give a voice for the voice less and the poor. I am motivated in my music career, and I hear a song that makes me want to just keep singing. I am reminded of how blessed I am to have a voice that I can use to sing and help others in the justice system". In the end, Carol Gonzalez is more than just another singer, she is a warrior using the talents she was given to open minds and fight for those in need.

C
A
R
O
L

Tony Curtis

Reggae-Dancehall Artist

In Ewarton, St Catherine, Curtis O'Brian (known as Tony Curtis to reggae fans) was born on beautiful September day. He grew up in Linstead, St Catherine with his mother, five sisters and five brothers; he still resides there when he is not on tour. His childhood was happy and fun with some of his fondest memories being the pranks he played on his grand dad and his friends. He visits his mother regularly and his father lives with him now. His humble beginnings inspired him to be charitable whenever he can.

Curtis says that becoming a musician was destiny because getting to know music did not take much. Finding a good producer was a challenge; producers and radio personalities were not always there when he began his career. He plays piano and guitar though he loves to hear drums and bass. Curtis describes his music as roots reggae and lovers rock – music that can touch the heart and soul. He enjoys performing especially when he can get a stadium to go wild and crazy for his music.

He loves that his music allows him to travel and so far, he has loved every place he's had the chance to visit. His family, his children and his close friends are his biggest supporters. While he has no regrets, he does have aspirations – he wants at least one Grammy award to put on his wall. All types of music are loved by Curtis but reggae is his favourite. He has been inspired by Bob Marley, Dennis Brown, Sanchez, and Sam Cook as well as The Wailers. He wishes that more conscious songs would be played on the radio.

Interestingly, he considers his biggest accomplishment not being music related but that of the roof over his head which he is so thankful for. He is also thankful for his life and his voice. Curtis likes to play Fifa Games and soccer in his spare time. Had he not been a singer, Curtis says he would be a soccer player or an actor. His favourite book is Seventh Child: A Family Memoir of Malcolm X. Curtis loves to cook what he terms as 'soul food' that does not have meat in it and he enjoys having his favourite fruits mangoes and oranges.

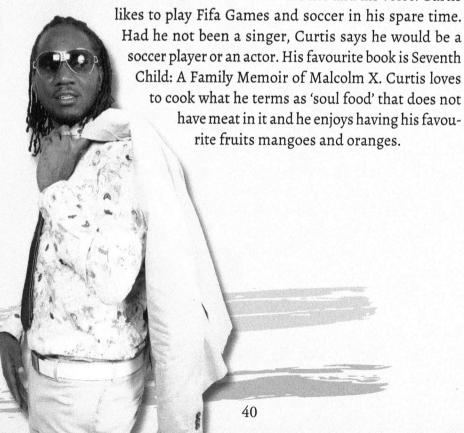

Blak Diamon

Reggae-Hip Hop-R&B Dancehall-Pop Artist

Shawn Anthony Myrie (you might know him as Blak Diamon) was born on December 26 in Kingston, Jamaica and grew up in the Havendale area. He was a very sheltered child, but his life was fun while growing up because he was surrounded by family, love, happiness, and music—always music. His parents are Rastafarians so during their prayers there was music, singing, instrument playing and the gathering of friends and family; all of whom came together as one to share in their spirituality, culture and knowledge.

Shawn looks on his childhood fondly and remembers his experiences growing up in a two parent household with his two brothers Jody and Andrew, who are the executive producers for their label UIM Records. Shawn's parents had him and his brothers when

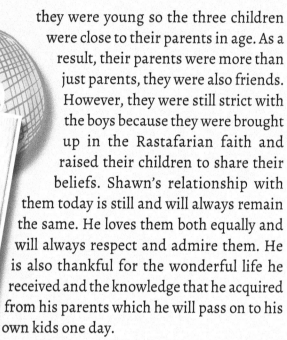

they were young so the three children were close to their parents in age. As a result, their parents were more than just parents, they were also friends. However, they were still strict with the boys because they were brought up in the Rastafarian faith and raised their children to share their beliefs. Shawn's relationship with them today is still and will always remain the same. He loves them both equally and will always respect and admire them. He is also thankful for the wonderful life he received and the knowledge that he acquired from his parents which he will pass on to his own kids one day.

Looking back, Shawn's fondest memory is of playing football and being the captain of his football team for every one of his schools from a very young age throughout his university days in Canada. He also loved to visit his family who were in the Jamaican countryside every summer holiday. It was a totally different setting from what he had in Kingston but the basic principles he had grown up with were still present such as family, spirituality and love. In the country everything was natural—natural foods and atmosphere—naturally, he loved being surrounded by nature.

Of course, the one thing Blak Diamon probably loves more than nature is music. He even remembers the exact moment he became interested in music. Shawn was in fifth form in high school and his dad got him a big pickup truck that had a loud sound system in it. One day, he was sitting in this truck listening to a Beenie Man song and all of a sudden, he heard something in the song he had never heard before—at least consciously. "I knew the song; I listened to it all the time. It was a feeling that just comes automatic without your knowledge. Sometimes when you are focused and listening to something you hear something different again in the beats. From that time, I was interested in the creation of music", says Blak Diamond. For about four years now, he has taken music more seriously and with every song he records, he grooms himself and his voice becomes stronger.

Nevertheless this incident aside, as we stated before music has always been a part of Shawn's life; while growing up, his parents were always playing various instruments. His mother is a poet so she was always writing and singing and his father played the drums. He taught Shawn how to play the Congo drums as a little boy. There was always some form of music around him at that period in time so it was somewhat "infused" in him from the start. Added to that, he and his brother had a sound system called "Uptempo Sounds." Before they knew it they were opening up a recording studio and producing music; Shawn realized that he enjoyed it. "I'm always making beats and sounds in my head. Anywhere! Everywhere! I use anything and make music. I'll use sticks and beat them together and make music," stated the talented artist.

Another thing that inspired Shawn to become a musician was God. "He gave me life. He gave me a talent. He gave me the very people who have also influenced me and continue to influence me throughout my life and career as a musician and as a man of this earth. I thank God daily for my family and my team because without them I wouldn't be here as Blak Diamon." His biggest supporters are his family, team and a few friends. From the beginning of his life and his career, he has been grateful to have these great people around him. They have all contributed to his existence and career.

With his supporters behind him, Shawn was able to become the great Blak Diamon; yet, one cannot simply become a musician overnight. There are certain things that have to be done and certain steps that have to be taken to become successful. There are always challenges. The steps Shawn took weren't easy, he and his team worked hard to get where they are now. The climb involved many late nights at the studio, sleepless nights, networking with radio DJs and selectors plus doing street promotions among other things. As well, the year Shawn started music fully his first two children had just been born (he now has five children). He was young, married plus balancing both a young family and a young music career. This was stressful because both required a hundred percent of his attention and time. There were other challenges as well such as; keeping the team together and focusing on goals to be accomplished. Funds were limited in the beginning and Shawn says that keeping the team motivated without pay was really hard; we can imagine just how difficult that was. Getting started was a challenge but nothing was going to stand in his way. "Challenges are what make me exceed and keeps me excelling. We all share the dream and we are getting more cemented in the industry and growing and learning both as individuals and as a group", Shawn said.

Shawn began his music career right after college without any vision but despite the challenges, he kept pushing on because he really loved music and wanted to produce it. Years of working and not giving up, led to his label becoming number one on the Island which is a great accomplishment. Also, he opened a concert for Ziggy Marley in Hawaii, performed at Hot 97 Boston Anniversary and did musical collaborations with Tommy Lee, Shawn Storm, Jadakiss, Yung Berg, Norris Man, Determine, Leftside, Bugle, Konshens and a whole host of other well-known recording artists. It takes a lot to rise in the music industry, but all of Shawn's hard work paid off and his music is now being played across the world in places like Brazil, Africa, Canada, England, Europe, and America. "It shows me that persistence, dedication, humility and fate brings results. If you want something you can't give up. You might be closer to getting it than you think. Listening to the radio and hearing fans speak about our work is just the greatest feeling in the world. Thank you Lord. I'm a step closer to my dream!" exclaimed the grateful Blak Diamond.

With all of these challenges and the grueling work eating up his schedule, where do things like hobbies and food fit in? When he is not playing his music, Shawn loves to play football as stated earlier and he even played it professionally until he was injured. In fact, if he had not become a musician, he would have pursued a career in football. Another hobby of his is cutting glass; shaping the glass and putting the pieces into frames— he also likes reading newspapers and the Bible. As for food, Shawn loves Jamaican apples and curry chicken with banana and dumplings,

which he says is the "baddest thing!" He has fun cooking breakfast foods like pancakes, bacon, eggs and French toast. Playing music while eating pancakes sounds like an awesome time, doesn't it?

Anyhow, being Blak Diamon has its advantages and he finds himself doing things today that he never thought he would do. When he was younger, he was very shy. Even in high school when he had presentations he would have to do it after class

45

with the teachers in private. He always thought he wasn't capable of certain jobs but now, he finds himself networking with many different types of people, even people who were deceitful and who he promised he would never deal with again. "I'm a strong person so there aren't many things that I say I wouldn't do."

Shawn's strength is not only beneficial to him but to others as well. He uses his strength and his compassion to make a difference in the world, not just with his music but with his heart. Recently, he sponsored a charity event in Cockburn Pen, Jamaica and he hopes to continue with it so he can see it grow and uplift the youths and the community. He would also like to open several other charities in the near future. Shawn gives the credit of his charitable spirit to God who inspires him to do helpful things. "If you are blessed and you can help you should; that's your blessing from God. I am very grateful for the life that God has given me. There are people who are unable to support themselves or their family so if you can help make a change then it's important that you do."

Not only does Shawn hope to change the lives of people like those at Cockburn Pen, he also wishes to see a change in the music industry. If he had the chance, he would change the structure of the music industry in Jamaica. Some levels can be tightened a little and some have to be completely restarted. One thing in particular that needs some adjusting is the radio. "The mentality of the radio hosts/personalities has to change. They abuse their power too often and do not realize the ripple effect it will have even on their own careers. We have to claim back our music too. Everyone else is benefitting from dancehall/reggae music except Jamaican artists. Clean it up and give the artists a chance. Everyone has a role to play in order for the thing to work. It's gone too far!" Blak Diamon takes his music seriously and to have to work in an industry that does not value or help its artists is upsetting for him.

Nevertheless, even if the music industry is a little messy, it won't stop Blak Diamon from creating the music that he loves. "The music I perform is the kind of music I like so it's good to my ears. There are messages in my music. It's conscious music. When you listen to my album, you will hear a lot more of these kinds of songs." His favourite song he has written is "In These Streets" because it is a real story about the worst point his life—a time when he just wanted to give up on music until something changed; thankfully he never did. Blak Diamon also has a favourite song to perform and that is "Life Too Sweet" because it has nice, happy vibes and is easy to sing.

Of course, as a musician, Blak Diamon does not only love to play music, but he also loves to listen to it. "My favourite type of music is real music—conscious music that carries a real message. But there is also a fun part of music that carries different melodies such as Michael Jackson, Sizzla and Bob Marley." He also enjoys listening to Richie Spice, Sizzla, Buju Banton, Jah Cure, Bounty Killer, Vybz Kartel and a few others. Shawn grew up in Jamaica so listening to dancehall/reggae music is a part of him. It's in his culture.

Shawn loves his career not only because he loves music but because even though it's a job, it is nothing like a regular 9-5 where you have to sit in an office or something of the sort all day. It offers him freedom to be flexible in order to do other things and to live at the same time. "To me, the career I chose put me on a level above other careers because I am the voice for a lot of people. Lots of people around the world are going to listen to my music and will be uplifted from it. Music offers me freedom to do what I want to do and to become someone great. I consider my career as God's choice, making me the voice to represent others."

Jah Rain

Producer-Reggae Artist

"What's in a name? A rose by any other name would smell as sweet" This philosophical reference was posed by Shakespeare years ago. Today, I ask the same question, what's in Umar Plummer or Jah Rain name? Would he be the same spiritually inclined, powerhouse of a musician he is today if he were called by another name? He would no doubt still be a talented roots reggae musician influenced by the likes of Bob Marley, Peter Tosh, Lucky Dube, Dennis Brown and Ken Booth.

This Kingston born individual was brought into this world on October 08, 1982 then raised in Car Hill and Rock Hall, St. Andrew. His spirituality is heavily embedded in his music and his view of humanity's condition

48

has heightened his awareness of the plight of others. This urges him to extend a helping hand wherever he can. "When I look at the vast amount of things that needs to be done to improve the lives of so many that are out there and are less fortunate, of them not having food to eat or a safe place to sleep at nights, that is enough inspiration to do charitable things" stated Umar. His compassion for others was instilled in him by his parents. They raised him to appreciate the gift of life which no material possession could replace and to live humbly. Umar recalls that life was not always easy. There were struggles and challenges but his positive outlook on life helped him to defeat these obstacles. He was particularly closer to his father, who always sought to teach him life lessons, ones that could not be found in the classroom. An ackee dish with some ground provisions can make him quite at home. He continues to reside in Jamaica while resting in between tours and hopes to have children of his own one day.

Being around nature and positive people that are self-aware is a great motivation that drives him to succeed but his greatest inspirations are his father and the creator. For many children their parents are larger than life. For Jah Rain, it was his father, Dyrick Plummer the musician, who surrounded Jah Rain with music from a young age. Starting in his father's band rehearsals; moving on to being interested in music himself which grew from making 'riddims' to singing. Music is his greatest passion. It has led him to achieve his greatest accomplishment in creating his band Jah Rain & The Iyah Vybz Kreation where he not only sings but jams on the keyboard. His performances and sound are often likened to Peter Tosh and Bob Marley. What a compliment! This roots rock reggae sound is synonymous with his roots and culture which embodies a soulful sound along with great songs, for example, Don't Burn Your Bridges are a part of his repertoire.

Though life has it challenges, his greatest obstacle has always been fear. "Living with fear is simple living with yourself and keep telling yourself that you can't is hard. When I realized that I over-came my fears I felt accomplished, it was and still is the greatest challenge I have ever overcome", states Umar. This extends to his pet peeve in the music industry. That focus seems to be on the love

for money and all it brings, but not the talent or the music. Regardless of the issues he continues to put his music forward with all the love and belief of his supporters behind him. His expression through this medium is an act of self-expression and freedom for him. He hopes his music sends a message to others to become self-aware and con-tinues to spread the teachings of His Majesty through song.

Jah Lex

Reggae Artist

Alex Corbeil was born on a most memorable day in Montreal, Canada. He celebrates his birthday on February 7th, so he was born in quite a cold, wintery time in northern hemisphere. Most of his time was spent in the city of Montreal and the summer months as a child he spent time in the country. Jah Lex only learned about his biological mother in his teen years. He loves both his mothers and since he moved to Jamaica in his early twenties, they visit him regularly over the years. Growing up in a loving household with the support of a hard working father and a loving mother enabled Jah Lex to see the world in a different way. He was in love with music from birth. Even though his father did not approve of his path, he eventually gave in when he saw how much music meant to his son. Due to his passion, Jah Lex's Aunt Chantal bought him his first electric

51

guitar at 11 years old. Interestingly, his grandfather is the only family member who plays a musical instrument, the violin.

Jah Lex's childhood was filled with laughter and amusement. His fondest memory is of spending good times with his friends in the back streets having lots of fun. Moving to Jamaica greatly contributed to inspiring him to create his very own music.

Music comes naturally to Jah Lex and he has loved reggae music right from the start so he is not at all surprised that path in life is that of a musician, particularly a reggae artist. He fondly remembers that music came to him from such a young age that he learned percussions before even learning to walk. That is an incredible musical feat right there. Jah Lex now plays African percussions, guitar, electric guitar, bass, trumpet and drums. He loves listening to roots and culture and has had this love from a very young age; he had a knack for Rastafarian messages in the songs he listened to. Pursuing a music career came to him on one fateful day when he dedicated all his time and efforts to fully realize his singing career. He felt, that becoming a reggae singer was his destiny and it became the driving force for him to pursue his dreams. Reggae music runs deep in Jah Lex's music career; Bob Marley, Burning Spears and Peter Tosh have played important roles in his youth as musical influences and continue to be a source of inspiration for him in the present time.

This child of the Most High loves to read and is also very mindful about what he eats. Two of his favourite books are "The Book of Psalms and Kebra Negast (The Glory of Kings)". He likes eating ortanique, banana and jelly, His Favourite dish though, is steamed callaloo mixed with other vegetables served alongside green bananas, dasheen, coco, and wheat dumplings. Typically a Jamaican soul, he also enjoys his early morning river swim. Honest and generous people especially those who care for the children are great in Jah Lex's book.

Being loved and treated as a very special person makes Jah Lex feel good about his music career. "Getting love and respect in the streets, those kinds of things make me feel a free man", said the artist. His success brings him a lot of good gifts such as fruits and vegetables from his farming fans; however, what he really loves the most about his music career is being able to "teach and touch people's hearts and souls through music." Being particularly close with Haile Selassie I, he has no regrets at all within his music career. If there is anything that he dislikes in the music industry, it is the producers and artists who lead the children astray by introducing slackness and negativity into their music. He wants to counteract this by showing good examples for the young.

He likes all genres of music as long as it comes from the heart; needless to say, he strongly adores reggae music and names Bob Marley as his top favourite musician and artist. There is no doubt that he infuses his music with the love from time-tested affinity with the most popular icon of reggae music. People sense it; they love his songs and this feeling of being able to give love to the others gives Jah Lex a sense of fulfillment that goes beyond reggae music.

Jah Lex performs music in the roots and culture genre. For him, it is the music that heals the world by sending out righteous messages. His favourite song that he wrote which he also loves to perform is Haile Selassie I. This loving soul is an active community member. He is a father of two children, a daughter and a son; aside from his fans, they are his biggest supporters and he considers them his prince and princess. He also loves the idea of getting married one day.

Needless to say, Jah Lex is very proud of his accomplishments in life particularly his music production and his music career. "Everything I have and everything I am today come from the music and Rastafari."

JAHLEXMUSIC.COM

Da'Ville

Producer-Reggae Artist

Da' Ville has been interested in music for as long as he can remember. In fact, his mother would always say that she could hear him humming from the womb. Having grown up in a musically inclined family, Da' Ville has always been exposed to music, but he has taken the art and fashioned it into something unique and individual to him. Looking back, he cannot imagine doing anything else besides making and playing music and anyway, can you even imagine him as a bank manager or accountant?

Da' Ville was born Orville Thomas on January 24 in Kingston, Jamaica. He grew up in different areas in the parish such as Tiger Valley, Oakland Crescent Kingston 11, and Hillview Terrace. For Da' Ville, growing up was bittersweet. He attended school like most children, attended church and had a few friends but, he didn't really get to enjoy a lot of things as a child. He was forced to grow up rather quickly because his father, a musician, was always away from home traveling. Being the oldest of his siblings, the responsibility of taking care of the family fell on him.

Not only did he have to take care of his siblings, Da' Ville did not have the luxury of growing up in a two-parent household; his father was never home and he scarcely knew his biological mother. He only saw her a few times. As a result, he was raised by his grand-mother until she died, after which he lived his teenage years with his father and step-mother. Not having the opportunity of living with his mother and father in the same household left Da' Ville feeling deprived of that gift. Not once did he ever felt loved while growing up and he remembers having an abusive childhood. For a long time that was all he could relate to; it wasn't until he reached his current age that he decided it was best to let it go. Fortunately, Da' Ville discovered God and music while growing up and those things helped in keeping him together. Despite not having spoken to his father in years, Da' Ville hopes they can one day patch up their relationship because regardless of everything that has occurred between them, he stresses how much he does indeed love his father. He yearns for a father-and-son relationship and prays that they can reach that stage one day. After all, his father played a major role in introducing Da' Ville to music.

Da'Ville grew up in a house surrounded by music. His father would always have music cassettes laying around the house which Da' Ville would find time to sit and play. It wasn't just reggae that he listened to, but also pop, soul, R&B, house, country, and even techno music. He was inspired by artists such as Michael Jackson, R-Kelly,

Maxi Priest, Lenny Kravitz, Maroon 5, U2, Usher, and Chris Brown among others. As a child, Da' Ville would take any opportunity he got to sing or play music, including singing in the church choir and in school concerts. He would even go to the recording studio with his father. In this way, Da' Ville learned a lot about music and it increased his passion for it.

Aside from his passion for music, Da' Ville has many other interests as well. He loves sports; specifically soccer, American football, and basketball. He can also be seen "kicking it" on his video games and going to the movie theater, restaurants, and comedy clubs. Da'Ville enjoys travelling and finds it uncomfortable being in one place for too long. In between travelling, playing music, and participating in his other activities, Da' Ville enjoys eating various kinds of fruits from bananas to strawberries and loves chicken cooked in just about any recipe. However, even though he is one to try new foods wherever he is, he classifies himself as a picky eater, it is important to note he does not eat red meat or pork.

Another interesting detail about Da'Ville are that he is a deeply religious person, and even his favourite book is the Bible, after all. He tries to read a verse or psalm every day which is very admirable. Furthermore, being charitable is something that comes naturally to Da' Ville. He feels the need to be charitable to those in need, especially the homeless because he empathizes with them as he too was homeless at the age of fourteen. He can understand what it feels like to be wanting for something and sometimes he even cries for the people he sees. He at times wishes he was able to give them some form of shelter and relief, thinking how fortunate he was to get out his own bad situation. Da' Ville is very thankful for every blessing he has received in life including his voice, his friends and family, his fans, and supporters.

Everyone has something that they like most about their lives and for Da'Ville; he appreciates the ticket to the world his career has given him. He has been presented with "an open window of endless opportunities" and the ability to sing and perform for people and make them happy. Being able to inspire people with his music is one of his greatest accomplishments. Of course he has some regrets, but, he strives to focus on the present and put the past behind him, even though it's rarely ever easy to do that. He states that everyone has regrets. It is a part of life so he tries his best to deal with them. He has had to overcome many challenges in his life and he has been faced with many people who insisted that he would never be successful. However, he didn't allow that to stop him from following his dreams and now he has countless hit songs and has been voted singer/vocalist of the year on various occasions. "I might not be the strongest, but I'm never too weak to fight and prove things to myself." With that attitude, nothing is impossible.

Gail Zucker Photography

Indeed, Da' Ville still has a long way to go and much still to prove to himself. He is still looking forward to being nominated for and eventually winning a Grammy (or even a few); meeting new people including producers and artists; learning new things such as how to play different instruments; traveling to new and exciting places and tapping into his greatest potential as an artist. He feels as though he still has much to do and discover about himself and his abilities and looks forward to accomplishing all of these things, hopefully with a family of his own to share them with.

Da' Ville has an unspeakable passion for music, a passion that drives him and inspires him to do almost anything. He sings for the world and his music seeks to reach people of all nationalities and backgrounds, inspiring people of all tongues and religions. Like all of the great musicians who came before him, Da' Ville's greatest wish is that his music will continue to thrive even after he is gone from the world. He believes that with the grace of God, anything is possible.

Adrian Xavier

Reggae-Soul Artist

Adrian Xavier Tremblay was born on December 13, 1974 in Seattle, Washington of all places; so how did this Seattle boy, a lover of coconuts, yoga, kayaking, and miso soup, even become interested in reggae music, let alone become a successful reggae artist? Answer: he had a lot of exposure to music as a child growing up in the mountains of Washington, as well as in Los Angeles, California.

While growing up, Adrian bounced around between his mother, who lived in Seattle, and his father, who lived in Los Angeles. He had many adventures traveling the west coast with his peace activist single mother, but his exposure to music came by way of his father, who was a DJ in Los Angeles and also worked with Rick Dees (a.k.a.

LA Larry) in the 80's. Adrian's father often took him to recording studios, which gave him insight into the world of the recording artist. Also, not only did Adrian get musical experience from his father, his godmother was an aspiring reggae DJ in Seattle and was a part of the Positive Vibes reggae show. With these kinds of family connections, he was able to meet Burning Spear backstage at UCSB in Santa Barbara and Dick Clark at a Michael Jackson concert. "Growing up around performers and the entertainment industry got it in my head early on that I had something."

It didn't take long for Adrian to discover a love for music and a dream of becoming a musician. He was very fortunate to have his supportive, music-loving family behind him (he credits his four sisters with the title of biggest supporters), as well as a wealth of other inspirational people to look up to, such as Jimi Hendrix, Bob Marley, Peter Tosh, John Lennon, and Ras Michael. So far, his career has been very successful and fulfilling. He has released dozens of songs, many of which he loves to perform; however, his favourite song he has written so far is "Good Thing." Adrian's music can be described as reggae world fusion that takes elements of soul, dub, hip-hop, and more to create a special sound. Most importantly, his music is uplifting with meaningful messages behind every lyric. "[The music] is all about a good feeling that connects with all people young and old." That's the most fulfilling part about his career: making people happy with a positive song.

Another thing Adrian loves about his career is the wealth of opportunities presented to him. He finds himself doing tons of things he never thought he would do, such as traveling to new places he would never have gone to otherwise, meeting interesting and exceptional people, and doing a lot of management work. He has no regrets so far and while he does wish he would have taken advantage of certain opportunities in the past, he is quite proud of everything he has accomplished. He has managed to remain an independent artist and who is innovative and dynamic. Adrian has learned to create opportunity and make things happen for himself instead of relying on other people. The endless potential of life, not to mention his love for music, is what drives him to keep moving forward.

Adrian Xavier is man with a deep love for community and family, including his three sons, and appreciates honesty and integrity above all in the people he meets. Also, while he plays four different

instruments, he considers his voice to be his "number one." Adrian is many things, but most of all, he is a musician dedicated to making meaningful, upbeat music for people all over the world. Who knows what fans will see of him down the road, but for certain they can expect nothing but excitement and of course, fantastic music.

Lance Sitton

Reggae-Roots Artist

Father, husband, son, brother, lover of Christ, and musician. All these capture the essence of Gregory Lance Sitton, a Midwestern American boy, infused with reggae in his soul. He has been playing music since he was 8 and he credits his mother as his greatest influence in becoming a musician. "She always sang and taught me to. I practiced my skills and writing and began pursuing it by playing as much as possible". Born on October 21, 1982 in Stillwater, Oklahoma, he's been playing music for 24 years.

Coming from a Christian background, Lance's love for Christ translates into doing what he can to help others by following God's example; and being thankful for his family who are his biggest supporters. An adventurous individual, Lance can be found out in nature battling the elements whether surfing on the seas or rock climbing. These activities provide the perfect contrast for the type of music he performs- roots reggae. Imagine if you can, a dark intimate space, with Mr. Sitton on the keys or maybe on the bass or guitar and let's not forget the drum. These are all instruments he has mastered, using them to; great beats, and feel good vibes in a chill atmosphere. He could be belting out 'Small Axe' by Bob Marley a favourite of his or even 'Good Vibe Music' one of the songs he's written. He has delved into the great musical goldmine of artists for inspiration and names Peter Tosh, Kevin Kinsella, Mat McHugh, Jack Johnson, Midnite and Jboog as some of his strongest influences. His career has afforded him the luxury of spreading a "positive vibe through music" and the ability to work from home which allows him to spend more time with his family in Springfield, Missouri. Who wouldn't love more family time?

Lance's childhood comprised of sports, music and love (not necessarily in that order). From church events, sports or music there were always a lot of activities he was involved in. His parents created a foundation for their family that is grounded in God. Along with his mom and brother, who are also musicians, they make quite a trio. Many of us have declared that we would never act like our parents only to still end up being very much like our parents. Lance shares this same sentiment but, nevertheless, finds himself acting more like his dad each day. Since becoming a father (to his son Kingston) and a husband, he cherishes the relationships with his parents even more. They are present in his life, giving parental and marital advice, and are involved grandparents who enjoy spending time with their grandson.

He takes solace in reading the book of Proverbs in the Bible. Keeping the words of wisdom from these pages in mind keeps him grounded and allows him to view things from a different perspective. Even though he has been burned by individuals he has invested in; he has decided to take these unfortunate experiences with a grain of salt and view them as a life lessons. Another person might have become jaded because of this situation but not Lance. He still maintained a positive outlook about the music industry by charting his own path and teaching himself what he needed to know about the industry which allowed him to be the self-sufficient individual he is today.

All these experiences went into creating his last two albums which landed on the iTunes reggae charts (#14 and #3, respectively), proving that hard work pays. Not bad for a boy from southwest Missouri. Taking a cue from these accomplishments, he hopes to push himself to the next level from #14 to #1 on the charts, improving his music and climbing v12. With such aspirations who could deny that Lance Sitton will undoubtedly leave a legacy in roots reggae.

David Dinsmore

Member of Judge Roughneck
Ska-Reggae Artist

David Michael Dinsmore was born on the 2nd of July, 1967 in Colorado Springs, Colorado. He grew up with his parents and his older sister in the suburbs of Colorado. He was a sensitive child who built tall walls to shield himself from emotional turmoil; however, they were not enough to protect him from depression at a very young age. Despite that struggle, as a young man in his school years, he was very bright, and exuded a strong self-image and a sense of originality.

His career started from the one of the most unlikely set of circumstances to ever shape a successful musician. While working at the Merry-Go-Round, a clothing store, in Colorado, he was fortunate to meet key personalities that ultimately sparked his interest in music. At this point in his life, he learned a lot about street life and he developed a love and appreciation for hip-hop, much to the dismay of his mother. Music then, became his catharsis and he gained much contentment from it. His immersion into music started his unlikely journey to becoming a successful professional musician in his own right.

Early on, his interest in music was nurtured by Mr. Combs, his Junior High School music teacher who put him in the jazz band. He took inspiration from late night jazz shows and in sharing the same interest with his friend Kent Stump. He later took trombone lessons from Mike Brumbaugh where he learned so much more about jazz music. He became so inspired by jazz culture and style that he started wearing bow ties and two-tone shoes to school and even took to speaking in jazz hipster slang.

What marked the beginning of his career in music and his love for reggae music goes way back in his grammar school, when he took an aptitude test and was found to be exceptionally attuned in music. This was the moment when he thought, "Yeah, I could get into this. I began playing trombone the next year and I've been playing ever since."

David's interests in life vary. He loves cooking and especially enjoys the challenge of recreating recipes of delicious food he's sampled in restaurants. He also loves the "Blood Meridian" by Cormac McCarthy, his favourite author. However, what really blows him away everyday are his two amazing boys, ages 17 and 13, who impress him with "how original and headstrong they are." His sons make him do things that he thought he would never do like, "I find myself turning my sons' music down. I wish it weren't true but it's TOO loud!"

Another interesting fact that makes David's music sound so full of life is his close relationship with his wife who is also his best friend. He takes pride in his faith and he values genuinely kind people. His biggest fans are none other than his wife and his two boys, who are his source of inspiration and encouragement whenever he feels like quitting. It also helps that his friend Vince has always been there for him, he has been his fan and staunch supporter for more than 20 years.

So far David's career has turned out great. He looks up to Ray Charles, Tom Waits, Miles Davis and Burning Spear who all provide him with an endless source of inspiration in the creation of his music. "Burning Spear live at Red Rocks could melt a heart of stone. The vibe is heavenly." David particularly takes pride in his "Purple

Dub" CD which "he arranged from the ground up, playing, singing and programming all the different parts." He then invited several of his musician friends to collaborate on the record and add more layers and textures to the music. He leaves his pieces open enough for his friends to be creative and "they usually come up with some pretty original takes on the classic songs from Prince's Purple Rain."

One of his personal favourites is the "Fire Come Down" from the Bow Shock CD "Sleepwalker" which he wrote and produced. Another one is an unrecorded song written in piano, called "It's all gone" which epitomizes all of his laments in life. Although, he has no particular song that he likes to perform, "playing live with Judge Roughneck is always fun. On trombone I get to improvise all night so it's always fresh. Byron is really generous with letting people stretch out and always mixes things up and keeps us on our toes."

David is a multi-talented musician who plays several instruments including; trombone, piano, and guitar. He also loves to sing and

rap. Although, he admits that he is a terrible guitar player because he started learning the instrument just a few years ago making him "an old dog learning new tricks." He plays mostly in the genres of ska, jazz, rap, and reggae. David is a deep musician and what makes his music stand out from the rest is the way he communicates to his audience. He tries hard to deliver a spiritual awakening to his audience; something that he could not explain in words, to him it's "just something about yearning and something about possibility."

What David loves the most about his music career is that it allows him to create music when he wants since he does not count on music to pay for his bills. He certainly treats it as his catharsis and this could be felt whenever he performs live. For him, the experience is simply surreal. "It's easy to believe in magic as a musician because magic happens all the time for you. You create it and it flows through you. 2 + 2 can equal 17. For those moments it feels like anything is possible."

David had found a good balance in his life, he is very active in his community, he holds deep love for his family, and he is able to indulge in his passion for music. He has no regrets in his music career but in his own words, "I wish there was a way to give each project all the love that it deserves. I have started a lot of really cool projects that I just can't give my all. I have just the one life!"

Like most contemporary musicians, he agrees that the music industry is too slow in recognizing the paradigm shift in music distribution. "While it is incredible to be able to get music directly to the listener, it has been difficult to in any way monetize it. Since cash liberates time, it makes it harder to find time to work on music as much as I would like."

David has so much more to offer to his fans. He has about 30 originals that he has yet to record so fans, watch out, there is more to come. You might find him playing live at the Paramount Theatre Colorado although he plans to play less live to get more work done in the studio.

Ted Bowne

Member of Passafire Reggae-Rock-Dub Artist

Reggae artists are beginning to emerge from all over the world uniting their varied cultures with the distinct sound and style that is reggae. Ted Bowne born 1983 in New Jersey, USA he later moved to the eastern shore of Maryland (Salisbury) when he was just 11 years old. After completing high school in Maryland, he relocated to Savannah, Georgia at the age of 18.There he went to Savannah College of Art and Design for Sound Design and graduated in 2006. Presently, he is a member of the hybrid musical band Passafire that brings both rock and reggae to the table along with other mixtures

of additional feel good genres and melodies. This was new and exciting venture, delving into reggae music. One might wonder how Ted found himself being drawn to a life of music? The truth is he was brought up in a family where all the members were lovers of music. His mother is a singer; his father is a piano player and his older brother's play bass, guitar and drums. This early immersion ensured that he would be a musical genius in the future. He credits his mom and brothers in encouraging his early interest in music. He describes his parents as being wonderful people who have always been supportive and understanding of whatever he wanted to do in life.

Like any other human being, Ted's life was filled with up and downs. He had a delightful childhood, the first ten years of his life he spent most of his days frolicking in the nearby woods and to him this was a wonderland for an adventurous young lad. He reminisces about the fun weekend jams that would take place at his house with his parents and family friends; they would play into the night and roast marshmallows around a huge bon fire. These and other memories help Ted to realize how blessed he was as a child. Unfortunately, after this happy phase, came a period of upheaval when his parents divorced. The years up until 18 years old were a bit hard for Ted as he had to move to another state and find a new school. For any child this situation would have seemed overwhelming and stressful, but Ted learned to see the positive in every situation.

At 12 years old he visited Jamaica, prior to the visit his mother had told him to bring items with him which he could trade for souvenirs. Surprisingly one day at the beach, a man was willing to trade some tapes he had for Ted's Troy Aikman Dallas Cowboys jersey. On these tapes were the songs of the legendary Bob Marley, from there Ted fell in love with reggae and decided to purchase Bob's album when he returned to the States. Ted was in various musical bands in high school including several different rock bands that would compete at their yearly talent shows. He then ventured off to college where his interest in recording music grew, he later got a degree in sound design and from there he decided that it was his destiny to be involved in the world of music. Today Ted enjoys listening bands like John Brown's Body, Giant Panda Guerilla Dub Squad, Seed, The Black Seeds, and Fat Freddie's Drop.

His mother, his rock, has always taught him to give back to society as one kind action can change a person's entire life. Charity and empathy are two key characteristics to have as a productive member of society. What Ted is mostly thankful for in life is being able to live in this generation which is filled with technological advances. He also give thanks for finding someone who loves and supports him unconditionally and allows him to love her in the same way, and last but definitely not least, he is extremely grateful for his interpersonal relationships with his friends and family.

Having a taste for Jamaican cuisine, Ted enjoys some delicious ackee and salt fish topped off with some good old scotch bonnet pepper. He also loves preparing his own family's recipe for apricot chicken. On days when he feels able to sit, relax and to enjoy a good book, Daniel Quinn would be his author of choice. When he feels like being active, he likes to skateboard, snowboard or surf. However, he prefers snowboarding and would snowboard whenever he gets the chance. Ted's positive nature drives him to seek out like-minded people who are filled with compassion, acceptance, tolerance and ambition. His biggest supporter was his late grandfather John R. Purnell who helped him through college and taught him how to have tolerance towards others.

Ted and his band were recently signed to Easy Star Records which is an American reggae label whose roster is full of bands such as: John Brown's Body, The Green, The Black Seeds, etc. What is really interesting is that these bands are among those that they have admired for so long which makes getting the chance to be a part of the family is a great accomplishment.

Like any rising sensation there were challenges that they had to face in the beginning. At first, the only places they could play were little bars in the southeast because they were unknown and were mostly occupied in the days by jobs and school. When they finished school, they went out to try and play at as many places as they possibly could. Their luck began to turn for the better; the first national tour became reality. After that, it was much easier to jump on national touring bills as an opener. The band now does national headliners and they are building strong followings everywhere. What Ted enjoys as a musician is that he is his own boss (along with his bandmates), they choose when to take breaks and do whatever they want to do. Ted acknowledges that he one day hopes to purse recording a solo album where he would play all the instruments. He would also love to produce a super successful album and get his name out there as a producer/audio engineer.

Ted's favourite song to perform is "Submersible" which the fans always seem to love. His favourite song he has written to date is "Feel It" which has reached the hearts of many individuals. Ted is a fan of 90's hip-hop and 70s roots reggae .He also loves soul, jazz and funk as well as Indie music. What Ted dislikes about the music industry is that the originality is slowly becoming a thing of the past. A lot what is consumed by the mainstream is recycled material. He realizes that we keep hearing the same beats, same chord structures, same themes and same subject matter. "When there is so much in the world to write about, why is it we keep reverting to singing about dancing, drinking and partying?" asks Ted. He also gets heated when he hears an artist singing in an accent or voice that is not theirs naturally. "Be you" is what Ted has to say to them.

What really drives Ted Bowne is this beautiful world with so many things to be thankful for. The opportunities that have been provided by his predecessors are too good to take for granted he believes. He is also driven by the rapidly changing world we live in and the intricate complexities of everyday life. He is indeed a true musician. He and his band will surely break barriers and continue to give the people what they love.

Harrison Stafford

Jazz-Reggae Artist

Jamaica has become the adopted home for many artists of different nationalities. They become immersed in the culture and are hooked by the beauty of the island, its people and music. Not one of the typical sun drenched beach boys from California, Harrison Stafford is one of Jamaica's adopted sons who is carving out a niche for himself. He splits his time between Portmore located in Jamaica and California. Born in Livermore, California in 1977, he grew up in Eastbay, California with his parents and older brother Jon.

Who would have thought a Jewish boy would embark on this Rastafarian reggae journey? Looking back, his entrance to the musical world was through the musical greats; the kings of pop and reggae, namely Michael Jackson and Bob Marley respectively. Without a doubt these musical talents made huge impression during his youth. His father, a jazz piano player, also peaked his interest in being a musician, along with Harrison's fascination for pianos. This musical aficionado became interested in pianos at the age of 4 and has been playing since the age of 8. He also added a variety of string and percussion instruments to his repertoire over the years. Following the example of the famed musician, Prince, he played several instruments through his entire album Natty Will Fly Again which featured Pablo Moses, Ashanti Roy (the Congos) and Winston Jarrett.

His interest in reggae goes beyond making music. He delves into the historical and cultural context of reggae music. In doing so, he is preserving the history of the movement for future generations. As such, Harrison participated in a documentary project entitled Holding on to Jah which will be released this year. It focuses on Rastafarian singers from the 60's and 70's including the visit of Hailie Selassie and the individuals that laid the foundation for reggae music in Jamaica.

With his family by his side, he continues to embark on his musical journey. He takes with him the bond and strength of his closest confidante, his partner, his wife. Harrison's love for reggae music manifests itself through yet another forum. As a rabbi, he taught a class called; 'Preserving the history of Reggae Music' at Somona State University of California from 1999-2002. The interest of persons in reggae from ages 18-60 was evident; so much so that he had to limit the class sizes. Now we can understand the power of reggae.

Harrison's love affair with Jamaica extends to its food, as well, with favorites such as ackee and salt fish or bread fruit with some curried tofu. Exercising is another activity he is involved in when not touring. A Herman Hesse fan he can be found with one of this author's books or playing a game of Glass Bead. Never one to only help himself, he gives back to the global community. "Music, reggae music is about inspiring people, donating your time, your spirit and energy. Due to this, we tour in places that are struggling to inspire them. People who are less fortunate."

Harrison had a typical childhood. From sports to the temple on weekends and Hebrew school in the evenings during the week. Coming from one of the few Jewish families in the area his only eccentricity may have been his interest in reggae. His family was a juxtaposition of the old mixed with the new. The Americanization of his parent's generation conflicted with that of his grandparent's. Love, laughter, music and religion were the order of his household. He maintains a close relationship with his parents who relish being grandparents.

As a white reggae band out of California, his band Groundation, had to prove they had what it takes to survive and gain respect in the reggae music world. A prophet is not honored in his own home town and this may hold true for them as they receive more attention outside of California. With rebel music as their battle cry, they felt drawn this innovative sound which inspires musicians to think outside the box. The sound of Groundation could be called a fusion of jazz and reggae with influences from the likes of Miles Davis, Bob Marley, Gregory Isaacs, Josh Hills and Peter Tosh.

An optimistic individual, Harrison visions of the future include freedom from oppression due to color, race and politics. Meeting new people and inspiring them to look towards a brighter future is just one of the many things he loves about his career. If not for this ability to reach people through music, Harrison would have been content as a professor. He gravitates towards individuals that are caring and unselfish; "we need to build up each other and all children of the world are ours". With zest and zeal for life, he lives it to the fullest, and hopes that others will experiences life as fully as he does.

Paul Anthony

Reggae Artist

For many great recording artists, the love of music is usually nurtured from a very early age and this was no different for Paul Anthony
Thompson II. Born November 8, 1989 in Palm Beach Florida, came
into this world, some would say possessing God given talents that
he would later use to rock the hearts and minds of people with sweet
melodies and life changing lyrics. People normally say if your job
is something you enjoy doing, you'll never have to work a day in
your life. For Paul, music was his hobby which transformed into his
career and that is something which is really inspiring. His taste for
reggae music really runs through the blood as his dad, Paul Anthony
Thompson Sr. (also known as "Pat Satchmo" in reggae music circles)
is a Jamaican vocalist and entertainer who shared stages with
acts from the great Bob Marley to the
"Harder They Come" artist Jimmy Cliff
and the beloved Dennis Brown. As a

youth he could remember watching his father cover hits like "Lady in Red", "Unforgettable", and "What a Wonderful World" which were some of his preferences.

Paul's life growing up was not much different than that of the average teen. He had two brothers and a sister and his parents got divorced when he was only five years old. Despite the separation, he continued to get the same love and support from both parents. His mother, originally from Canada later remarried. He described her as a very organized, compassionate, creative and kind-hearted woman who pushed and inspired him to do better in all he does. He cites this as one of his biggest motivations to become a better artist and a better man each day. Like any other caring mother, she felt that education was important. This encouraged Paul to pursue his bachelor's degree which he received in 2011.

Reggae was his first love and from there dancehall and hip hop became his crushes. At only twelve he was encouraged by a classmate named Aris to write his own original lyrics. In no time he recorded his first song which was entitled "Nuff Gyal". He then ventured on to write and perform his own music at multiple talent shows around South Florida as a "Reggae-Rapper". At age 16 he then formed a hip-hop/R&B/reggae infused super group (urban boy-band) with some close friends called 5th City, to which he contributed the reggae element and spice. The group remained together for a couple of years and started to generate interest both locally and nationally. Several managers approached the group with management deal offers but they were denied due to dappled contracts.

At 18, Paul decided to venture on his own as a solo performer and the group disbanded peacefully. Paul later signed to a record label out of Fort Lauderdale known as "Fire Star

Entertainment". With the help of his former manager, "Trak Magic," he was able to secure major radio airplay, national and international performances and increase his fan base by the thousands. At age 21, with the help of Jamusa who is a radio deejay and reggae music veteran, he was able to make a big splash on the reggae music scene. By his virtue, he appeared in various festivals such as Jamaican Independence Day, One Love Reggae Festival and Caribbean Unifest among others. He also had a single, "Girl," featured on a VP Records Mix CD Yesterday & Today which was very popular in Jamaica, the US and England. Today he is a self-managed, professional musician/ songwriter making a decent living. Just recently he has crossed paths with legendary reggae band Inner Circle who have been helping Paul to further cultivate his talents at their facility Circle House Studios in Miami. He credits all the people who took a chance on him, and especially his family, in being where he is today. His future only looks brighter!

Questions may be asked how such an artistic talent was fostered. The truth is as stated above; Paul was always surrounded by music. His father as we said before had great connections in the music arena and worked with Lee "Scratch" Perry with whom he released some successful hits on the Upsetters label that did well in Jamaica and abroad. HIs father then moved to the U.S. where he also achieved success, singing at the Apollo Theatre in NYC and traveling to Canada, Connecticut and Florida performing at various hotspots, sharing his impeccable talent with the masses. Paul describes his dad as being a friendly, hardworking and generous man. He has managed to use his talents to do what he loves, while supporting his family to this day.

Wait though, the awesomeness doesn't end there! Paul's stepfather Jamaican born Maurice Walker also has an ear for music. He described him as a brilliant musician producer and one of the most renowned bass-players to come out of Jamaica. Mr. Walker has done production work on tracks for many artists such as Dennis Brown and Horace Andy. He has helped to guide Paul musically by teaching him music theory, keyboard and how to operate recording software/ equipment. Paul gives his respect to his stepfather whom he said is very intelligent and has offered him a wealth of knowledge and wisdom on every day aspects of life.

His family inspires him mostly to go out and go hard in both his personal and professional life. With his kind heart and positive mind Paul sees charity as something that is to be encouraged even if it's an individual or a small group because these positive energies will begin to spread like ripples and will help to bring about change for the less fortunate. He believes positivity is the key, and love is his inspiration. Seeing all the unfairness, disunity and pain in the world softens his heart and influences him to take part in charitable events. Paul is always thankful for the simple yet great things in life such as health and his family, his gifts and his talents. When Paul is not touring you can always find him in South Florida, you know what they say "Home is where the heart is". The young artist does not have a specific favourite dish as he believes the category is broad and he loves all variety as long as it is delicious but he does have a taste for mouth-watering Jamaican dishes such as stewed chicken, oxtail, jerk chicken and fish. He also enjoys Chinese and Latin foods. His favourite writer is J.K. Rowling, even though he is not currently much of a book person, this is something he plans to change in the near future. Becoming a family man is one of Paul's lifetime wishes; being a good father is one of the things which he feels would make him feel more accomplished.

One thing Paul dislikes about the music industry is when true talent is overshadowed by mediocrity and unsubstantial shock-value. Often times he sees talentless persons rise to the top with no hard work and who, in his opinion, add nothing of value to music. He sees things like this as a slap in the face to him and other good, hard-working artists who actually pay their dues. There are artists who seem content to focus on shallow inconsequential matters which distract the public from real issues going on in the world. Paul believes the agenda of the "Bigger Heads" is to dilute our consciousness, which is why he believes it is important to make conscious music. "Bob Marley did it and so will I" he added.

His most proud accomplishment is his latest release *Light After Dark*. It was his first project that he had one hundred percent creative control over and he recorded and mixed it on his own. The concept of the album is one that he is very pleased of. He explains that *Light After Dark* comes from the idea that no pain is ever permanent. All struggles are temporary and there will be brighter days ahead. He made this album with the message to give people hope of happiness on the other side of whatever misfortune they are going through. He later took it a step further and allowed his fans to choose their own pricing of the album and he promised to donate half of the proceedings to charity. He was able to donate a substantial amount of money to Food for the Poor, a charitable organization which is geared towards helping less fortunate people of the Caribbean.

Like most artists, Paul is grateful for the chance to uplift and change people's lives through music. He is aware of the influence music can have on a person, which is why he continues to produce positive music; and strives to motivate others for good.

Despite various ups and downs throughout his life, Paul uses music to release his innermost thoughts and feelings. He says heartbreak has inspired him to write some of his best material. Regardless, he believes love is the meaning of life and we as human beings must actively seek it out. Paul's biggest challenge has been earning a living while continuing to pursue his music career. It has been a very rough and rocky road but he is finally beginning to reap the fruits of his labor, "I am at the point now where I am making my living doing music, however, I am continuing to remain humble and acknowledge the fact that I still have room to grow", he said. Paul aspires to win Grammys someday as he views this as a strong indication that an artist is on the right track in their career. His favourite song which he has written is called "Brown Eyes,", featuring his father Pat Satchmo which is also his favourite song to perform. Another song he enjoys performing is "Welcome to Jamrock" by Damian Marley. If it wasn't music, Paul says his career would have been teaching. He loves to pass down knowledge to those willing to receive it.

This fast rising artist Paul Anthony Thompson II is on his way becoming one of the great pillars of the reggae music community!

Granville Campbell

Lyrical Tenor, Classical Artist

JAMAICA CALLING

GARCIA

GRANVILLE CAMPBELL

Granville Campbell, at 51, is still an indispensible ingredient of any important concert in Jamaica.

Born in Spanish Town on October 7th, 1892, he showed unusual musical ability at a very early age, and for several years was principal boy soprano at the Cathedral. Later he returned as leading tenor soloist, and for the past thirty years his name has appeared in the programmes of all the important musical events in Jamaica. Few people hearing him sing would guess that he is entirely self-taught; he has developed his talent without the benefit of any tuition. Since the earliest days of ZQI, he has been heard in regular song recitals, and has recently turned his attention to composition. His setting of "Jamaica Arise" is well known, and "Glorious Jamaica" with words by Jim Russell, first heard on Monday, June 21st, seems destined to take its place with the best songs to come out of this Island.

He is at present engaged on his "Mass in C" which will be heard for the first time of the coming Silver Jubilee.

Jamaica has produced many great musicians in the 20th century. I'd like to shine the light on one such artist that history has forgotten, Granville Campbell, a self-taught classical tenor and lyricist who is also the author's great-great grandfather. There has been no real mention of him since the death of the late Prime Minister, Norman Washington Manley. It is time to reintroduce the greatness of Granville Campbell to the land of his

82

birth and the rest of the world. He was highly sought after vocalist and received many accolades for his vocal performances.

Life is not measured by the number of breaths we take, but by the moments that take our breath away. Before reggae music or Bob Marley and the Wailers, there was Granville Campbell a musical genius who sang classical music and swept the country off its feet with his golden voice. Born on October 7th, 1892 in Spanish Town, Jamaica, he started playing the piano at approximately age four and began to sing within the church. Granville was an altar boy and a faithful member of the Roman Catholic Church. A master of music, he composed many songs and paid tribute to his religious upbringing as a Roman Catholic by writing a Mass. He was the voice off the inspiring political songs for the People's National Party, Jamaica Arise and Glorious Jamaica. Mr. Campbell was also co-composer of the PNP's song, Land of My Birth.

"He enjoyed widespread fame throughout Jamaica as a singer and was hailed as one of the most talented musical performers that the country had produced along with three other gifted musicians of the day - William Spooner a bass singer, alongside Mrs. Steadman and Mrs. Lopez who sang contralto and soprano respectively - he made up a famous quartette that sang brilliantly from classical and semi-classical music. They were in demand for concert appearances everywhere in Jamaica. At the zenith of his career, he was the leading soloist of the Diocesan Festival Choir, the leading choral group of Jamaica whose annual recitals were the high-water mark of the musical year in Jamaica", ___this information was contributed by Mr. Jim Russell the Daily Gleaner reporter of that era. Granville was s show stopper, even garnering the reputation of lover boy due to the copious amount attention he received from the ladies. His voice so pure it made everything around him come to a standstill when he sang.

Good music over centuries is said to possess charms that can soothe one's soul and Granville had the power to create such music. Mr. Campbell combined his love of music and his desire to teach music to others; inspired him to start a music school where piano and other music lessons were taught. He was an accomplished pianist who believed that giving every child the same opportunity, whether they rich or poor, helped them to stay out of trouble. He believed in their God-given abilities and wanted to nurture their talents.

In 1946, Granville made his first trip overseas to Panama with pianist Lois Kelly (later known as Mrs. Barrow). He scored a single triumph, particularly among the Jamaican-Panamanian community there. In 1949 he migrated to England with his family. He may not have been at the height of his musical prowess when he left for England, but he was still able to leave an indelible mark on the musical landscape there. His talent later extended across the waters to the United States where he migrated once again in 1959 to be with family and there he continued his singing career.

"A naturally gifted tenor with remarkable breathing control and enunciation, he was considered to have had the potential of world renowned accomplishment had he gone abroad earlier than he did. He continued his musical career, doing concerts and also serving as a member of a noted choir - that of the Church of St. Mary the Virgin, in New York." (Jim Russell)

After 13 years of not appearing in Jamaica, Granville Campbell came home to triumph in 1962. An invitation was extended to him and many other notable citizens by the government to take part in the Independence Celebrations of Jamaica. He sang with the Jamaica Military Band at an independence concert, gave a broadcast recital over J.B.C. (Jamaica Broadcasting Corporation) and appeared at private soirees. Once again the golden voice that had thrilled thousands of his fellow Jamaicans in the earlier part of the 20th Century was heard in the land - the lilting tenor that never failed to stir his native audience and move them to a storm of applause.

He was a great singer of light and semi-classical songs. Especially popular was his rendition of I walk Beside You, the great wedding classic. One of Jamaica's great singers during the 1950's was Jimmy Tucker, a young man at the time who sang with Granville. Heather had the pleasure of speaking with Mr. Tucker, who was quite shocked to hear from a member of Mr. Campbell's family. Mr. Tucker had this to say to her, "You brought back some of the fondest memories of my life when you mentioned Granville Campbell. He was a great tutor, a leader and a humble man. The biggest part of my life's work entails the life of Granville Campbell".

"He contributed to music, several beautiful waltzes of the earlier 20th Century, the words of which were written by Astley Clerk and balladeers of that period. Granville appeared in concert programs throughout Jamaica in churches and elsewhere. He was the forerunner of the classical concert as we know it today and made a great contribution to Jamaica in preparing the public for appreciation of classical music. Mr. Campbell's presentation of these easily understood harmonious songs of minstrel texture was warmly appreciated and he helped to familiarize the Jamaican ear with the semi-classic then classical music." (Jim Russell)

He often appeared with another great Jamaican singer of that period, Sgt. Major Spooner. They both enhanced the musical landscape of the time.

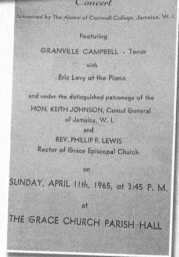

Seeing life through an artist's eyes comes with many challenges but also many great rewards. Before his death in 1968 at the age of 75, Granville still had many fans, young and old, around the world who loved his music, personality and humanity. Mr. Campbell had an extensive family including 15 wonderful children with his first and second wives, as well as, several grandchildren, great-grand-children and other family members. Jamaica serenaded him (Tribute to Granville Campbell); a piece that can be found on Jimmy Tucker LP commemorating the late artist. He was self-taught, which is something difficult to do as a classical singer; this makes his success even much more admirable.

Classical music has the power to move human minds and spirits positively. Classical music affects the brain's organization and abilities through its melody and rhythm. The rhythm raises the level of serotonin produced in your brain. Serotonin is a neurotransmitter involved in the transmission of nerve impulses that helps maintain joyous feelings. This is why some credit classical music with being able to help overcome depression. Melody and rhythm are the two essential components of music that works in very different ways; melody is the essence that boosts creative reasoning, while rhythm synchronizes these emotions with the vital patterns.

Jamaica, arise, let's give tribute once again to a legend, and a great contributor to the "land we love", let us celebrate Mr. Granville Campbell.

Csavi

Producer-Reggae Hip Hop-Dancehall Artist

Born on October 23rd on the sweet island of the Grand Bahamas, Shavon Mitchell naturally had a feel for reggae music. The cool and relaxed environment of the Bahamas clearly contributed to her amazing music career. Her exposure to music started early on at the age of 5 when she started playing the keyboard. However she remembers that everything became clear to her when she was 11, thanks to her mother who gave her plenty of cassette tapes to listen to. She recalls annoying her siblings during a car trips when she would take control of the radio from the front seat where she played, paused, rewound, and played again and again all of her favourite songs. This was later cemented by her first stage experience in her sophomore years.

Csavi grew up in the central part of the Bahamas together with her siblings and her parents. Both her parents have excellent taste in music and they both dreamt of reaching for the stars but because of financial circumstances, they had to put the welfare of their children first instead of pursuing their dreams. Her father is a religious man and she adores his sense of responsibility. She likes the humorous personality of her mother and her attitude towards cleanliness; Csavi remembers cleaning the house even when there was nothing to clean. The prominent figure that really helped Csavi discover the musician in her is her grandfather, John Grant. He sent her to music school and helped her to start her career through financial support. He even converted his shed to be her temporary studio when she was just starting her music production.

Her parents gave their dreams of pursing music and instead chose to devote their time and efforts to their children. The sacrifice has inspired Csavi and has given her the determination to one day put her lineage where it truly belongs — in the long line of popular musicians. This goal has enabled her to work harder and strengthened her resolve to succeed. She also claims a "divine inspiration" finally showed her that music is her life's calling. She worked so hard that she spent many sleepless nights in the studio mastering her craft. She remarks; "I went from production, to writing, to composing, to arranging, to rapping, to background vocals, to singing and engineering, artist development and the list continues". It is evident that a lot of sacrifice goes into this career. Time away from family, friends, and social life takes a toll sometimes but it is all worth it." Just like her father, Csavi puts God above everything else. Her music reverberates a divine influence that she shares with her audience indirectly. She wants to make a difference by doing what needs to be done right now, she is not going to wait for success and fame. Her attitude towards music is driven by an authentic passion for what she truly believes in.

Csavi loves movies, going to the beach and also traveling to different places to sample different cuisines, to enjoy the local flavor of music and culture, and to observe the native scenery and landscape. What she loves about a person is their ability to be respectful, understanding and most importantly honest or simply being real around her. She doesn't want the company of people who waste her time by being jealous and not offering genuine support when needed. Csavi would love to get married and have children one day. The idea of starting a family actually inspires her to do more; "I want to be able to tell my children stories about myself and also let my children read about what their mother did and is still doing."

Another interesting thing about Csavi is that she enjoys cooking for others, but when she's by herself, will often indulge herself with a pizza and some sugar apple. When she has time to cook; she makes nice cocoa dough, which happens to be her favourite cold morning dish while reading. She doesn't have a favourite author or a favourite book necessarily, but she likes reading lots of exciting biographies.

Csavi is very close to her family and missed them greatly but since her career debut she has started to pull away from them in order to continue realizing her full potential. Part of the problem is the dissension in her family around her decision to pursue a career as a musician. While her grandfather fully supports her career and goals, her father always wanted her to use her degree in music to teach at schools in order to have a stable career. She realizes that this may not be the healthiest way of dealing with things, but it is a way of coping that has made it easier for her to travel for her long periods and focus on her career.

In the end, Csavi's career turned out just fine and her grandfather is very excited about her music production, which is now taking off. She is very proud of this achievement. She believes that for one to live a happy and fulfilling life, one must understand his or her own existence. Csavi shares her deep insights "I started living when I started to understand who I am." She understands that she disappointed her father by not abiding by his wishes and in following her own dreams. Although, in the end she is very proud of what she did. She states; "A lot of people are unhappy because they are living someone's dream, maybe what their father or mother want them to be but not really what God created them to be." Csavi enjoys doing what she loves the most — music production.

It is interesting to note that Csavi did have her share of rough patches in her pursuit of a career in music production, beyond those in her family. Of course, no one ever said that the path to success would be well paved and comfortable. The particular challenges she met in her career were the people that held her back. In the end, she is grateful; "It's amazing how God allows other people's plans of destruction for your life to turn out into success. I guess it's as if you're intuitively connected to see an oasis in the desert." She also finds gender to be a difficulty in the music industry because men tend to be intimidated by women but she's grateful that she was able to lay down a good foundation for her music career in spite of these hurdles.

Certainly, Csavi loves working with talented people all over the world. This broadens her understanding of music even more and enables her to help more musicians. Helping musicians realize their potential brings Csavi a great sense of pride. Some of those she groomed are now successful and are already performing all over the world. If she were not a musician herself, she would gladly be a multi-millionaire who helps start-up musicians.

Nonetheless, Csavi continues to strive for personal development. "I want to keep expanding, learning and prospering in all that I do and inspiring the masses to do so as well. This leads to success in all other areas; mentally, emotionally, physically, and spiritually."

Peter Runks

Reggae Artist

The song "Can't Keep a Good Man Down" could very well be the soundtrack to Peter Runks' life. Born November 12, under the given name Tawanto Saunders, in New Providence Bahamas and now married with three kids of his own he looks back at his childhood and the road he travelled to be where he is now. Raised by his grandmothers in Bimini, he was hardly around his parents. Seeing the destruction drug abuse can cause he channeled his grief in writing songs. Using a school program as his forum to hit out against the use of drugs, he wrote a rap against drug abuse. He was a hit and since then music has been his calling. He recalls that at the age of 10 he became interested in music and since then he has been performing and began playing professionally in 1995.

The circumstances surrounding his childhood made him shield his children from his past experiences. Being able to provide for his family; buying them a home and sending his children to a great school are what he's most proud of. His career to this point is more than just making music. It is about giving back to the community. His grandmother was a charitable person and seeing her give of herself inspired him to do the same. He points out that "one can't be successful, unless you give back" and as such hopes to start a foundation that helps children to realize their potential.

The music industry can be a hard business at times. The atmosphere more often than not is permeated with making the bottom-line and not the message in the music and this bothers him. He hopes to shift this attitude by continuing to be positive and singing uplifting lyrics. No doubt, he has experienced his fair share of challenges and negativity. The lack of unity and support when it comes to a new artist can be devastating and can end a career before it begins. He found this to be true and more prudent to produce and make his own music. With this respect, he remains true to himself and continues to support those who come after him.

Music runs deep within his family, especially on his father's side where there is a producer and an artist named Ramzez DaRuler. We can see how this may have influenced is path to music. No doubt, roots reggae is his passion influenced by artists such as Mikey General, Dennis Brown, Chronixx and Luciano. Through this medium he developed his sound. A message as old as time singing good will, with positive sounds to all people. Witnessing the reactions of fans to his music is always a priceless moment. The song he's most fond of that he has written is "Mama I Love You" and he values

his relationship with the group Culture Shock Reality and holds their friendship as an important aspect of his life and musical journey. His family and his fans continue to be his greatest supporters on his path.

Just as his songs bring clarity and seek to effect change so are his choices of reading materials. He is often found with books by Steven Corey or re-reading the "The 7 Habits of Highly Effective People". Peter also enjoys listening to Dr. Myles Munroe, a mentor and a leader for many. In an alternate reality, Peter Runks is a mechanic, and a man of many skills. His hands are just as talented as his vocals; he loves to fix and create things with his hands. After tinkering with the electronics, he enjoys eating some pork chops and an apple which does him well. He is comfortable around folks who are true to themselves and appreciates; individuals who aren't afraid to speak up. Life may have dealt him a few dirty hands but Peter Runks refused to be defeated. Instead, he adapted to the circumstances and took it as a life lesson. He uses the love of his family to push him; "to keep making a difference and making a change despite the negative sounds around me".

Onesty

Reggae Artist

From dancing to rapping to being a reggae singer, everything has come full circle for Tina Sureda Castello. She claims more than her fair share of musical talent in her family with several aunts and uncles who singe and a sister who plays violin; Tina now working under the stage name Onesty, has paved her way to becoming a great reggae artist. As one of the first reggae artists from Belgium in the underground reggae scene, Tina as experienced her share of ups and downs in order to be where she is today.

Born in Antwerp, Belgium, Tina spent parts of her childhood with her aunt and then grandmother in the center of the city. Tina and her siblings Elissa and Vincent were raised by relatives because their mother was ill and unable to care for them. Her parents had been separated by the time she was four, however, despite these early challenges, her childhood was a happy one. The vacations she spent in Spain with her family are happy memories filled with peace and warmth. She points out that growing up in Europe you can find yourself on both ends of the spectrum. The socio-economic benefits are wonderful but the cold climate can keep people apart and to themselves. Her grandfather's story shows the strength and determination one must have when the odds are stacked against them. Her grandfather, Juan, and his brother fled their native country of Spain and came to Belgium to escape from the unrest that was taking place at that in Barcelona. They travelled by bicycle over the mountains in France to eventually settle in Belgium. This sense of determination and strength has flowed from that generation onward and now to Onesty.

"Everybody has to do good for others. I don't see any point in a life that's only built around me", states Onesty. The ability to do good for others and making the world better one person at a time is a part of Onesty's mission. Contributing to Green peace and lending her support to benefits has allowed her live out that sentiment. She has been actively pursuing music from the age of 6 when she joined a church choir. The name Onesty came about through one of her "partners in rhyme" at that time. The name resonated with her and she uses it as her foundation to build on.

The road to bringing the Onesty name to the world has been a very eventful road for Tina. Starting out with a passion for writing and dancing she connected with people who were in hip hop music. This segued into creating a rap group called Antwerp Finest, under the name MC T. She was the only female MC in her town at that time. Not one to sit and wait for things to open up for her she sought to create opportunities for herself. She organized her own Open Mic events and placed her rap crew in the lineup. Then by chance she met a reggae band and within months was touring Belgium. Now singing reggae music, she resolved that she needed to learn from the best and so she journeyed to the birthplace of reggae Jamaica. Since then she's been travelling between Jamaica and Belgium. The final pieces of the puzzle fell into place when she met Marcia Simpson and Jermaine Forde, who became the final members of the Onesty team.

Tina is the proud mother of a three year old daughter to whom she dedicated the song "Life Starts". Her daughter is the most special person in her life and is counted amongst her mother and the Onesty family who are her greatest devotees. Though her passage as not been an easy one she tries not to dwell on regrets. "Regrets always come too late, they don't make you feel good, it doesn't help you so I try not to regret anything and just deal with things, turn them around". The Onesty sound is about positive music and messages, and about tran-scending genres. This includes live music with real instru-ments with the Onesty twist without any pretenses. Being in love and mending heartbreaks are also apart of Tina's experi-ence which makes her music and songs relatable. She's not only a lover of humanity but also a lover of stewed chicken with yam and boiled dumplings. Her passion knows no bounds and she is still an avid dancer. Her focus and her dreams have brought much hap-piness to her life without which

she would be lost. She uses this to drive her to excel and accomplish her goals one of which is to gain a bigger audience and platform.

The Tina you see today is not the same Tina from a year ago. She may have made some miss-steps in the past which she refuses to remain focused on the past. Instead, she chooses to remain positive and focused on her current and future projects. She is thankful for the opportunity to work with the right people who share her vision. She perseveres by releasing anger from her life with her mantra, "anger frees the way to inspiration and wisdom". As such she values people that are humble, respectful and understanding, and those who continue to be positive throughout adversity and never give up.

Mikey Dangerous

Reggae-Dancehall Hip-Hop Artist

"It's all about music. Music sets me free."

For someone who rose to success from the ghettos of Kingston, Jamaica, reggae artist Mikey Dangerous proves that a dream and a passion can be enough to get you over the toughest of hurdles and leave you with no regrets. In fact, Mikey celebrates the hardships he had to go through because according to him, they made him who he is today and he is proud of himself.

Music had always been a part of Mikey's life but; he never imagined himself becoming a musician/performer. If he wasn't a musician today he would most likely have become a professional soccer player or auto mechanic. Nevertheless, we are all lucky that Mikey found his way to music and this happened because he didn't like to play soccer in the winter.

When Mikey moved from Jamaica to Montreal, Canada, he began playing soccer like he had always done in Jamaica. However, he found it unfavorable to play soccer indoors, so once winter came, what else was he to do?

The answer came when a family member asked Mikey to be the opening performer in a show he was organizing. Of course, he always knew that he could sing, however, performing live didn't really interest him, or at least, he could never imagine himself doing it until this opportunity arose. After his performance that night, he recognized and accepted the musical talent he possessed and so did the people who saw him perform. After receiving much praise for his performance, Mikey's musical journey began to take off.

Entering the music business can be intimidating and challenging, so it helps to have a handful of supporters to make the experience a little more bearable. For Mikey Dangerous, his support comes from his parents, four siblings, and close friends. He describes his parents as hardworking and very supportive of his talents. Also, even though his father had migrated when Mikey was around five or six years old and therefore not around, he maintains a close relationship with both of his parents today, as well as with his siblings.

Mikey gains inspiration from a handful of idols, including his soccer coaches and fellow players; however, most of his inspiration comes from musical artist Shabba Ranks. Shabba was the one who inspired Mikey to begin singing in the first place and ironically, it was on Shabba's show that Mikey made his first live appearance. One of the moments most highlighted to peak his interest in music was when he saw Shabba arrive at a show by helicopter transport. Mikey describes the experience as "Maaad!"

The best thing about a career in music is getting to travel and meeting a whole new world of people. Mikey appreciates the unique opportunity he has been given. His favourite aspect of choosing this career is being able to experience things he never would have otherwise, such as winning a Juno Award in 2008. The Juno award is presented annually to Canadian musicians of all genres. This accomplishment showed Mikey that hard work and dedication leads to success and as much as he has succeeded in, there is still much more to accomplish. In the future, Mikey hopes to achieve more number-one spots and to complete his first album.

Mikey's music can be described as reggae on another level. Whether it's cultural reggae or dancehall, it will always be associated with feel-good music that people can appreciate and enjoy. The vibe and flow of his music comes to him naturally. He loves to share his songs with others, especially his favourites "Don't Go Pretending," (for which he achieved the Juno award), "Higher than High," "The Only One," and "So Proud."

Music is Mikey's soul but most especially reggae music. In actuality, he loves it so much that his only complaint about it is that the people who benefit from it are not Jamaicans who created reggae music in the first place. He wishes that reggae artists were more appreciated and recognized. It is for this reason and others that he is moved to do charitable things. According to Mikey, it is very important to remember where you come from and to appreciate the people, places, and things that helped to shape you. Yet, Mikey is charitable by nature and he always looks for ways to give back to people, especially the less fortunate.

Mikey is thankful for everything he has received in life and everything he has accomplished. But most of all, he is thankful for life itself. "Once you have life, anything is possible. Once you have life, you can be thankful for everything else," declares the devoted artist. Every day of his life he proves that he knows how to make the most of it and he has made the most of his career. Music is what drives him and inspires him. In fact, he cannot imagine his life without music. "I am music, if I don't sing, it's di saddest thing," says Mikey.

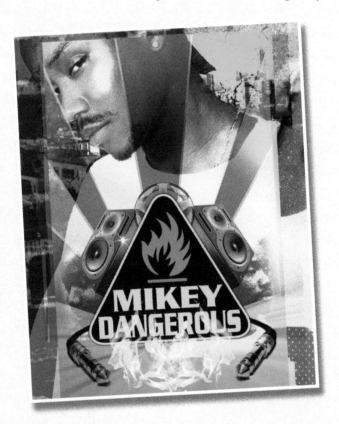

Black Prophet

African Roots-Rock Reggae Artist

What do you get; when a street kid who grew up in Accra, Ghana gets a hold of reggae? You get Kenneth W.Z. Bossman aka Black Prophet. Nothing beats a story; where the transformative power of music changes the life of an individual and sets them on a noble path. Kenneth Bossman was born on March 4th, 1977. The tragedy surrounding his childhood only adds to the inspirational rise of this

Ghanaian, turned reggae artist. Growing up on the streets provided some early lessons in survival and these street smarts would serve him well as he grew up. Performing from the age of 8, he used his talent to feed himself by serenading the market women as well as performing for the immigration officers in order to be able to cross the borders of Ghana's neighboring countries. Life was hard, but Kenneth views many of the hardships he encountered as life that have made him into the person he is today. Although he had no parents, he had a sister and two brothers as companions throughout his earlier years.

Through the guidance and inspiration of Jah, he held on to music as a sanctuary. His musical talent has taken him from the market place and streets of Ghana to main stages around the world, taking him far beyond his wildest imagination allowing him to travel and to speak his truth. Through his gift of song and reggae music he has been able to "share music, inner feelings and my message to people around the world." Like most of us, he has loved and lost but admits that it is a part of life. His mission as a reggae artist is to, spread his music to foreign countries, and ultimately to help and inspire people who have faced similar challenges to his own. He is

indeed a reggae artist to the core; he draws inspiration from artists who have made enlightening and inspirational music that uplifts the world. His sound is a unique blend of reggae music with traditional African elements and a rock influence. He points out that the fusion of these varied styles makes his sound "very vibrant and interesting". I think his numerous fans would agree. He finds that the music industry can be fickle and unfair: becoming a big artist is not indicative of how talented the artist is but is underscored by a fat bank account and who you know. This realization pushed him to create his own record label called Prophetic Music Production where talent could thrive and shine. Throughout his journey, he has faced numerous challenges but he uses them as stepping stones to get where he is today with his biggest supporters at his side: his fans.

So what compels this man to give back to those less fortunate? The powerful line of the song 'Masses' which he wrote: "When the leaders get greedy and selfish I want to know who suffers the most? –Masses! Masses!" Oh Lord 'Masses' recognizes the injustices that rage within today's society. Drawing from the hardships he went through as a child allows him to see from the perspective of those who are less privileged. The need to help those who cannot fight for themselves because of the obstacles stacked against them compels him to give back.

For this vegan, being a traditional herbalist would have been his calling if music wasn't his first love and so, one would find him creating healthy vegan dishes when not making music. One could call him the jack of all trades when it comes to instruments because he is adept at playing "a little bit of everything". When not travelling he spends his downtime between Ghana and Germany. He may be the only musician in his family, but his determination has enabled his talent and message to spread worldwide. His favourite song to perform is "African Leaders" which is directed to leaders in his homeland. His sympathetic and empathetic nature draws him to individuals who are hardworking, respectful and humble. Prophet has no regrets and with Jah's blessings and unconditional love for mankind that drives him; he will continue to spread his message of love and equality for all.

Jermaine

Producer-Reggae Artist

Jermaine Brinsley Forde, born in St. Mary's Hospital on April 5, 1975 in London, United Kingdom is a drummer, pianist, bass and guitar player and producer. When he is not travelling, he lives in his birthplace London. If not a musician what would he be? When asked that question, the reply is there is strong chance he would have become a pilot. Forde loves to do many things, but what he loves the most is to make music. Of course, what else can you expect from someone who claims to been born with music in his bones?

Growing up as a child, Jermaine's days were very fun and adventurous—filled with the excitement of travelling and the joys of meeting new people. His childhood was also filled with music since his father; step-father and uncles were all musically inclined. He had every opportunity to develop his musical gifts and to gain an appreciation for the one thing that would later define his career.

Where, in fact, did Jermaine's interest in a musical career come from? Well, his cousin Mark was the first to introduce him to idea of music as a career, of course music lessons helped a lot and he gained a lot of experience by going on tour with his parents, as well as listening to other artists such as Black Uhuru and Aswad. Nonetheless, his main source of inspiration comes from his parents and family. With ten sisters and six brothers in his corner, there is sure to be no shortage of support. Speaking of support, Jermaine says that his greatest support comes from his mother and his wife.

Earlier in life, Jermaine had not thought that he would have ever gotten married; in fact, he often declared that he never would, so it is ironic that he now finds himself with a wife whose love and support he cannot imagine being without. He finds that she is one of the dearest people in his life and he is very close to her. Today the couple have five children; two boys and three girls. While Jermaine finds it challenging to balance working other jobs to provide for his family with his musical career, he is very thankful for his family and their constant support.

Support from loved ones can go a long way, especially for one such as Jermaine, who possesses an ample amount of ambition and a drive to succeed in everything. One of his greatest hopes is to one day have a single reach the Billboard charts. Jermaine wants his lively and spiritual reggae/dancehall music to reach people all over the world; he wants them to really enjoy themselves while listening to it just as he enjoys creating this music. Furthermore, Jermaine loves performing his music for others, especially because he gets to travel to different places which he believes is one of the best things about his career. One of his favourite songs to perform is called "Just One of Those Days," and his favourite song that he has written is "Got to Get Your Love," which he wrote with his dad.

Jermaine has been making music for over 25 years and he shows no signs of stopping or slowing down. He really enjoys his career even though he expresses disappointment that his music is not selling as well as it used to. He continues to seek creative ways to address these issues and hopefully he will succeed, but meanwhile, Jermaine presses on with his music. He is obviously a very charitable and thoughtful person who seeks to fix a wrong whenever he can. "As long as there is evil it inspires me to do good," says Jermaine. He gets this strength of character from his mother whom he describes as very kind, loving, as well as ambitious and strong-minded. Together they operate the reggae focused establishment Ajang Music Production.

So far in his career Jermaine has no regrets or inhibitions about anything he has done, save for the fact that he wishes he hadn't let certain obstacles get his way along the road. He loves reggae music and he loves what he does, so as long as that passion remains, any further obstacles that come along will be worth the hurdle.

Sebastian Sturm

Reggae Artist

Germany has produced a number of reggae artists. The reggae culture has become prevalent there in recent years, leading a new wave of young people interested in expressing their thoughts through this genre and Sebastian Sturm is an exceptional example of German grown reggae artist. Now living in Aachen where he was born, which is 15 km away from Eschweiler the town in which he grew up he remembers playing in the woods with his best friend during the summertime. A

childhood that was innocent and carefree filled with promise and excitement. In Aachen, he was born to an Indonesian mother and German father on April 27th, 1980. His family continues to be his central focus and maintains strong relationships with his parents and elder brother as well as his band mates. If he ever needed an extra hand in his band he could use his family members as they all play an instrument or can sing. His daughter plays the guitar, wife with vocals and his dad on the keys. He may have the qualifications of a design-assistant but he never expected to become a reggae-singer.

Known to wield a reggae guitar and reggae bass, invoking melodies and beats that are pleasing to the ear, Sturm strums to the beat of his-own music. Throughout his early teen years his taste in music was on the punk side, but these days it's the vibrant sounds of reggae that moves him. The defining moment that catapulted him towards music was at the age of 13 when his brother showed him how to play chords on guitar during a summer vacation on the island of Nias while visiting his grandparents. After returning from vacation a fierce competition ensued after he found out some classmates were learning to play the guitar as well. He credits this experience along with the creation of his first band in drawing, him to music.

A basketball fan to the core, Sebastian can be found throwing a few hoops during his downtime. He also enjoys cooking one of his specialties is preparing a steaming bowl of spaghetti Bolognese. His eclectic taste in food will have him craving for Jamaican mangoes, pineapples from Thailand and bio-apple from his native Germany. Sturm has a healthy appetite for books and so he reads just about anything he can get his hands on. He's not only a musician, but also husband and father. These are roles he not only cherishes, but are most thankful for, along with music of course. His career has allowed him to be creative and, express himself through his music; he has also been fortunate to meet people and find interesting collaborators, all of which have added immensely to his life as a musician. The adventures and challenges make it even more worthwhile.

Making mistakes is part of the journey, but for Sebastian, there are no regrets. Each choice he made has led to the opening of one door and the closing of a door another, all the while keeping him on the path he has chosen, in pursuit of music. Ultimately, they have led him to this point and he contends that "I am still alive and I'm still doing my thing". There may be no regrets, but there are certainly issues within the music industry that bother him. The main issue is the practice of downloading or streaming music for free on the internet, "there are many things in the music industry that I found weird and smelly, but I think the worst thing is that you could get every kind of music for free (If you want). That means as musician you can't count on selling records anymore. And that's really sad, because time, money, maybe trouble, sweat and tears, hopes and dreams and of course much love are inside every record (even if you don't like the music!)". This is also his greatest challenge to making a good living with his music.

However, Sebastian continues to push the boundaries of his career by working on extending his fan base around the globe. His first gig outside of Europe was in Jamaica this year and he hopes to perform in more overseas. The inspiration for his music comes from the greats such as Bob Marley and the Wailers. He is wonderful songwriters, as well; his favourite songs that he has penned are "Get Going", "This Change is Nice", "Real Strength" and "Faith". Through his music he has had the opportunity to help whenever he can, however he can.

Uwe Banton

Roots-Reggae Artist

Hailing from Lage/Lippe, Germany there is no doubt that 'Uwe Schäfer' a husband and a father of three, known to the reggae fraternity community and his beloved fans as 'Uwe Banton', is another great 'roots rocking' reggae artist who brings good vibes and positive vibrations to his conscious lyrics and heart felt melodies. On a great November 28th day marked in history, Uwe Banton made his way into this world. He was the 2nd child for his parents out of four boys. Growing up in a small village located in the countryside of Germany where there was river and lots of lush green vegetation, one could imagine that these pastoral landscapes of Uwe's youth tied in nicely with his affinity for a style of music that is well known to promote nature and natural elements. He grew up with his parents who he described as loving and supportive, unfortunately the union between his mother and father came to an end when he was just 15 years old. The upset caused by his parents' divorce led him to seek comfort elsewhere, as a result he found; strength and a sense of happiness in that 'sweet sweet' reggae music. The desire grew stronger in Banton, to make his own feel good reggae music and from then on, the rest was history.

As a child, like most young boys, he was first inspired by his father. As he grew older, he started studying the lyrics and messages of the legendary Bob Marley and other great artists. This led to Uwe becoming more involved in the Rasta phenomenon as he started to read deeper and expand his knowledge about Rastafarianism, Haile Selassie and life as a whole.

Things that he is really thankful for are the precious gems of this earth. He enjoys being able to share love with family, friends and other people and last, but by no means least, to have the gift of music to share with people around the world with the hopes.

Venturing into his personal likes and dislikes there are some pretty amazing facts about reveals some interesting tidbits about Uwe. When someone has a taste for a wide variety of food it can be hard figuring out which dish is their favourite to prepare, this was true for Uwe. He loves cooking in general, especially Asian style vegetables. Some of his favourite fruits are mangoes, sour-sop, strawberries, raspberries, pineapple and grapefruits. He has no particular favourite author, but his favourite books are the Bible and the Kebra Nagast. Apart from those two, he enjoys reading books that are based on facts, such as auto biographies, books about nature and history books, whether political or religious. Apart from singing and writing songs, Uwe enjoys photography and likes to edit his own photos.

Like many artist, Uwe has his own contentions about the music industry. What he isn't fond of about the music industry is the declining quality of music that is considered marketable for big recording labels. "As a musician, naturally you believe in good music and its impact, so there were times when we used to believe that if you were only to do your best, then one day you would be recognized by some A&R guy from some major label or big record company. Later, we got to learn that it has by far more to do with what big labels consider as marketable in terms of potential sales. Because of the involvement of mass media into marketing music the industry seems to have gone more and more into easy marketing music. Which does not necessarily mean the best of musical quality, but rather what sells best", Uwe stated.

Uwe Banton is a person who likes to associate himself with people who has good traits such as being honest, caring, respectful and relaxed. This man promotes charitable events with a fullness of being; it is essential for him to contribute and participate in charitable events. Uwe often reminds himself that there is so much more to life than merely earning money and accumulating wealth for the benefits of one self or ones family. He believes in unity, people coming together despite their differences. While his biggest supporter is his family, when Uwe feels like he needs to find his inner self and meditate on important issue he turns to Jah for guidance, thus, he would often go out for nature walks to find his balance.

In his life's journey he doesn't believe in regrets, mainly because the hands of time cannot be turned to alter the past. In the long run, these experiences informed his life in ways he is thankful for. He is thankful for his inner voice which he found through faith and reggae music. As Banton presses on to higher heights in his career, one of the challenges he has had to overcome as an artist is learning how to market himself in this modern age of technology; via the internet and through social media. As an independent artist he thinks that it is the most important thing to know how to take advantage of these modern tools. When looking back at his career, he acknowledges not only his successes but also recognizes the sacrifice and hardship he went through to get there. What he admires about himself as an artist is that he is able to be creative and express himself through his work. Uwe is able to travel a lot and explore places many people don't get a chance to experience. He also enjoys the freedom of being able to work based on his own initiative and drive. "The financial income of an artist is very unsteady and depends very much on live engagements; sometimes even has some very rough time periods to bridge when "nuttn' nah gwaan" (nothing is going on). "That is why when asked 'who is your biggest supporter?' I have to say my family, because they are there for me by my side to go through thick and thin" Uwe reassured.

For his career goals he wants his music to soar to new heights, break down barriers and overshoot boundaries which in turn he hopes will enable him to help people financially. He gives hats off to other great artists who have inspired him such as: Aston and Carlton Barrett, Earl "Chinna" Smith, Monty Alexander, and Carlos Santana. Many musicians he's worked with have also inspired him, including Jamaican born Ras T.K.U. Eitiko Tafari, who was a great musical tutor to Uwe Banton, imparting knowledge about music, harmonies and how to arrange a song.

For Uwe picking a favourite song to perform is rather difficult task, since all his songs have a special meaning to him. His music is a type of from-the-depth-of-his-heart-and-soul-music which would appeal to anyone who allows the music to take control.

What really drives Uwe Banton? The fact that David slayed Goliath with one stone and a sling; this means anything is possible.

kanabiz

Reggae Artist

Reggae transcends culture, class, race and nationalities. It speaks to people across the globe with its positive messages. The connection was made with a child born in Colon, Panama. His parents, named this child Roberto Alexis Rodriguez Cordoba and to his fans he is known as Kanabiz. Hailing from an alley in Colon named "Callejon Martinez"; Roberto grew up determined to follow in the footsteps of his older cousin, Jose Solis, who was a renowned Dj. Roberto's cousin became his link to music and stimulated his interest in this area.

Kanabiz has been in the music business for 26 years both as an amateur and a professional singer. His professional debut was in 2005. Since

then he has written favourite's such as "Cuando una mujer se enamora" and performed songs such as "Voceros de la paz". It has been an odyssey for Roberto one fraught with regrets and challenges. Being the benevolent person he is, Roberto assisted may thought out the foundation of his career but it was never reciprocated. During his pursuit of his music he had to pull his family apart in order to accomplish his musical goals. That was just one, of the many challenges he had endure. Roberto has two daughters, Lia Nicole and Nayarith. Kanabiz states, "I am a societal person, but I am not that close to people. I love being around people but, I am somewhat of 'a loner', and I do miss my parents and daughters." From his experience he sees, "that the top artists are not famous because of their talent, they are famous because of the money they spend on their managers; it is pretty hard to change that problem." Kanabiz continues to give back to the world and causes to save the environment and helping foundations against violence. There may have been many glitches along the way but his career allows him the freedom to do what he wants and how he wants to do things, in order to help make a difference.

Roberto grew up with his parents and siblings; he was raised in a loving environment filled with companionship. Watching music videos of reggae artist was as much a part of his childhood as the sports activities he participated in daily. Living in a middle class family where would he get exposed to these reggae artists at such a tender age? This is where having a huge extended family can be a great advantage. Just as cousins normally borrow and lend each other their possession, a relative lent Roberto a series of videos of reggae singers and this unwittingly sent him on the road to realizing his dream. The videos opened his eyes, mind and creativity to another world entirely, filled with expectations and he began to seek and learn more about reggae for himself.

His quest and journey led him to becoming the artist known as "Kanabiz". When his music inspires others, it breathes life into them, his lyrics elevates to a higher level. It elates him knowing people admire his music and dreads too. He's not only a talented singer but also plays several musical instruments: such as guitar, piano, bass guitar and percussion. His family lineage is bursting with musical talent, such as: Tony Cheng, a winner of 2 (OTI) awards; Johanna and Reynaldo Rodriguez, they play the saxophone, Dj Boff, a producer, Manuel De Jesus Abrego, a accordionist, and José Manuel Rodriguez, kanabiz brother who plays lead guitar in his reggae band called "Ragamuffin Style" which consist a rough sound with lots of drums and bass. He draws inspiration from reggae, ballads and from musicians such as Red dragon, Cutty Ranks, Bob Marley and Manu Chao. He remembers the moment he got hooked on reggae as clear as if it were yesterday. Listening to his tape of "Chicho Man" one of the first Spanish reggae singers.

This Panamanian may be a renowned artist but his taste for food is simple. He favourite fruit is papaya, and he loves oatmeal and enjoys cooking pasta. The potential comic artist relishes performing in front of a crowd, feeding off the energy they give; it fills him with gratitude and an indescribable rush. Although he was born in Colon City he now resides in Panama City where he hopes to establish his own music label one day. His respectful nature and morals which were taught by his parents are an integral part of his character. They reflect the respect, tolerance and sincerity he hopes to see in all humanity. Kanabiz is not only good with his instruments but is also an avid gamer. His PlayStation system is a constant when travelling. He is very good at the sports, water polo and swimming. He enjoys reading "Cortos para Reflexionar" by Jorge Bucay or anything for that matter by author Osho. He writes blogs on the internet and plays soccer. Truly, he is a man of many talents.

Richie Campbell

Reggae-Soul-Dancehall Artist

Ricardo Ventura da Costa known as Richie Campbell and his music described as reggae with a touch of soul. Born on November 25, 1986 in Lisbon, Portugal, Campbell has loved music for as long as he can remember, but it was at the early age of sixteen that he began his music journey when he started a band with a group of friends. From that moment on, he has been making music that inspires the world with meaningful and uplifting messages. Reggae has become a very significant part of Campbell's life and he hopes that one day his music will captivate audiences around the world.

Campbell grew up with very loving and supportive parents along with his brother. His father was a self-made business man and provided his family with all the essentials they needed. Campbell wishes to encapsulate a balance of their character within him. He is very thankful for his family, especially his mother who is his biggest enthusiast, alley and tower of strength, and he is grateful for everything provided spiritually and physically. In fact, Campbell's favourite childhood memory is family-related and involved the whole family gathering together on the weekends and just enjoying each other's company. Campbell hopes to one day make a family of his own and while marriage is not quite on his to-do list at the moment, he does wish to have children. Family is very important to him and it continues to be the driving force behind everything he does.

For every musician there is a muse that gravitated them towards music, for Campbell, it was all the sounds combined to make sweet music. I used to sing all the time and from there I began writing a few songs." Campbell was also motivated by some great musicians like Alton Ellis, Luther Vandross, Stevie Wonder, and Marvin Gaye. He was captivated by their mesmerizing voices and wanted to sound just like them.

Campbell says his job is his favourite hobby, making music. His favourite food is chicken and enjoys reading Plato, Socrates, and Martin Luther King, Jr., while creating music and performing for an audience brings him great joy. His favourite song to perform is "That's How We Roll" because he enjoys the crowd's response to it and the reaction is never the same, which always blows his mind. However, even though he has a favourite song to perform, he cannot choose his favourite song, since they all have a special message, which is an impossible thing to do. "That's like asking a father to choose his favourite son!" He likes various genre of music for different reasons, but the songs he likes most are those whose lyrics convey a strong statement.

Of all the things Campbell has accomplished in his music career, he is most proud with his music video "That's How We Roll." The video has reached over one million views and this feat is a confirmation for Campbell that he has a seat in the music industry. With this triumph under his belt, he cannot say that he has any strong regrets about where his career has taken him. While he does wish he could have taken music more seriously at a younger age, he is satisfied with all of his decisions that have led him to where he is today.

Despite not having any regrets about his career, the music industry proved itself disappointing especially when it came to reggae music. As most reggae artists can attest to the fact that reggae music didn't and still hasn't been given the exposure and props that it so richly deserves, the stigma that surrounds reggae music displeases Campbell in many ways. "Reggae music has its own language," he stated, "it has the power to build and break, reggae music is one of the most influential genre in the world. "This is something we need to do together and that's the biggest challenge because there is a lot of ego in music, and too much of it is in the reggae business."

However, regardless of how other people view reggae music, Campbell values every second he gets to spend doing what he loves. He cannot imagine what his life would have been like should he have pursued a career in anthropology, which he had actually gotten a degree in before he made his big break in music. Music has become his life and has allowed him to meet a variety of people with different educations, religions, nationalities, etc... From his career, he has developed a greater understanding of people and has received a gift of being better able to appreciate, tolerate, and accept everyone as an individual. Music has opened up his heart, mind and introduced him to things he never could have imagined before. His career has encouraged him to become a more charitable and compassionate person, and in the future, he hopes his music will allow him to better himself further as both a person and an artist. Campbell wants to make a difference in the world through his music because that's just how he rolls.

Dactah Chando

Reggae Artist

Fernando Bethencourt, widely known as Dactah Chando, is a unique reggae artist. He was initially unfamiliar with this particular style of music, since he is not from Jamaica. However, once he was introduced to reggae he felt a deep connection to it and was drawn to the essence of this music. Chando was born in Santa Cruz De Tenerife, which is the capital of Tenerife Island, of the Canary Islands. Chando grew up in the rural mountains of Anaga on the north-east section of the island, where he lived with his parents, two sisters and one brother (who is also a musician). His childhood was spent in a quiet village, isolated from the chaos of the city; his environment was ideal for farming, fishing, running through the mountains with friends, and occasionally dabbling in music (in Chando's case it was bit more than dabbling).

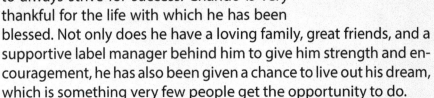

Dactah Chando started playing music at a very tender age. As a child, he was always in the presence of music because his father, a goat shepherd, liked to sing and play the guitar. In fact, his father was the main source of inspiration both musically and in life. Chando's parents were excellent role models for their son and encouraged him to be a great individual and to always strive for success. Chando is very thankful for the life with which he has been blessed. Not only does he have a loving family, great friends, and a supportive label manager behind him to give him strength and encouragement, he has also been given a chance to live out his dream, which is something very few people get the opportunity to do.

Music is very important to Chando, especially reggae music. According to Chando, his music is "a kind of deep-bass, all-styles reggae" sung in the Spanish language with a conscious message and heavy beats. "I think my music is not only great because of me but also the production work and those I have working tirelessly with me to bring out the edge and suave that is needed." Chando has released many songs, but his favourite song he has written to date is "Power Fi Chant," and his favourite song to perform is "Mantente Firme." Not only does he write amazing songs, Chando

can also plays the guitar superbly, and is proficient on the bass, drums, and a few other instruments. He plans on learning how to play even more musical instruments, and wants to learn more about music techniques. Chando finds himself doing a great deal of unexpected things, such as "singing different music styles" and "playing some new instruments." He has accomplished much in his life, despite some external and personal challenges, such as fighting to be himself and follow through with his dream to becoming an elite and a very talented musician.

So with all that under his belt, who is to say he won't accomplish any goal he sets his mind on. Even with such a strong mindset and drive to succeed, he could not have become the artist he is without some sort of inspiration. While much inspiration comes from his family, Chando is also inspired musical geniuses such as Peter Tosh, Bob Marley, Joseph Hill, Winston Rodney, Vaughan Benjamin, Dezarie, Ella Fitzgerald, Nina Simone, Lucky Dube, Bill Withers, Marvin Gaye, Kurt Elling, Sly Dumbar, and many more. Chando said "when listening to these artists, I am transported back to my younger days when I first dreamt of being a musician. I am truly appreciative and thrilled that my music is able to touch the lives and hearts of these young people today." In fact, that's the most rewarding part of his career being able to inspire people of all ages everywhere around the world with his music and the messages behind the music.

Chando values honesty and positivity, especially when it comes to music. If there was anything he could change about the music industry today, it would be the negativity that can sometimes pervert it. He wants his music to have a positive impact on people—he wants it to inspire them to follow their dreams and be the best people they can be. "We need more positive music, and positive artists. One must be honest with themself [sic] and with the audience, in all aspects of music and message."

Dactah Chando is an artist, who not only values the music he plays, but also hopes for something good to come out of his profession. He wants to foster positivity in the minds of the people who listen to his music, and hopefully though the messages embedded in his lyrics, impact the injustice and negativity in the world in a meaningful way.

And through everything, whether he is sitting at home in Tenerife Island eating his favourite food, avocado; cooking his favourite soups; surfing, hiking, or reading his favourite book (which just so happens to be the Bible), Chando is always connected to music, especially reggae, which may not be a popular industry where he comes from, but it is where his heart lives.

El Ganjoman

Reggae Roots- New Roots Dancehall-Latin Artist

El Ganjoman was born Leandro Numa Rojas Hernandez on January 11, 1989, in Caracas, Venezuela. He lived there for eight years before moving to the state of Monagas where he lived until the age of fifteen. He grew up with his parents, a brother and a sister. He keeps a fairly close relationship with both of his parents; they see each other as often as possible.

He fondly remembers his father singing and playing instruments, this was what sparked his interest in music. El Ganjoman's father gave him his first musical instrument, a "Cuatro" (A Venezuelan stringed

instrument), then later gave him his first guitar and taught him how to play chords. El Ganjoman's mother has also been a great motivator, she loves to sing and she is also a teacher. His parents and brothers enjoy making music, not as a career but as a hobby. In his teens, he was inspired by all of the bands and musicians who he listened to at that time. His interest in music flourished as he got older, he proceeded to play more frequently and slowly formed his own band with his friends. Everyday thereafter, he began to fall more and more in love with music.

El Ganjoman enjoys all genre of music, from blues and jazz to rock and hip hop. He is also a lover of Latin music like salsa and bossa, but the music he enjoys most is "Jamaican music," from ska, through rocksteady, up to the reggae which is the style of music that represents him. The musician who most inspired him throughout his career is undoubtedly the great Bob Marley, both musically and personally.

One of his biggest challenges he has faced was recording his first songs. He spent years composing, and then had the opportunity to use a studio; there he recorded his first demos. Following this he slowly started to spread his work and he even got a part time job to pay for his recordings. This time was a little hard for him but it taught him resilience and to work hard to achieve his goals. When he began he never imagined doing music as a singer but after spending a few years and seeing the potential it had, he became the singer and composer of all of the songs that he plays today. He has been playing professionally since 2009 and has no regret thus far. Today, he dedicates himself a hundred percent to his music, since 2006, he also founded a recording studio and music production called "Venezuela Ghetto Youth," and currently studies in the college of music "Jose Angel Lamas."

One of the most important achievements for him was finding Venezuela Ghetto Youth, knowing how very expensive to record and produce a good song in Venezuela. He now has the opportunity to work in a more personal way with his music, making all musical arrangements plus mixing and mastering. One of the main reasons for establishing the recording studio was to support those who don't have the resources to pay. El Ganjoman co-worker, friend and brother Monte Carlo works together at Venezuela Ghetto Youth.

He is currently working on what will be his first album in combination with Monte Carlo under the production of Mr. Dalis Sadman. The two are also working on the promotion of their music; they want to reach all corners of the world and continue to spreading their message of peace, unity and brotherhood.

El Ganjoman believes that in Venezuela there is a lot of rivalry and competition between musicians and bands. He also believes that music can achieve many positive endeavors such as bringing people together enabling to sow love, peace and happiness. When he does charitable acts, he considers it a way to contribute to society and to give back as much support as he can. He thinks if we can help and assist the needy, the world would be a better place.

What El Ganjoman enjoys most about his career is almost everything because he loves what he does; it has been very important to him since the beginning because he enjoys it a lot. His passion and love for music has led him to where he is today. Now that music is his source of income, remembering that he loves it makes the job less stressful; it keeps him cheerful and positive. Mr. Hernandez is proud to be able to travel outside of Venezuela to play his music, to share with other world-renowned musician and to have fans around the world. The greatest support he gets is from his fans; he is very grateful for all the support that he receives daily by all the people who connects with his music - people of all ages, from children to seniors.

He has many favored songs which he has written, one of which is called "Inspiración" (Inspiration), which he wrote for his daughter's mother. Two songs that he enjoys performing live are called "Cultivando Voy" (Cultivating) and "Combination" because when he sings them, they convey many emotions that people identify and connect with. His main instrument is the guitar but he also plays the Cuatro, keyboard, drums and bass. Music composed by El Ganjoman has very strong influences of reggae and Jamaican music which he merges with his Latin roots. If he was not a musician, he believes that he would still be working in some music related field,--perhaps as a sound engineer, a producer or something of that sort.

In his teenage years, Ganjoman's heart was broken by a handful of women so to speak. So out of that lesson learnt he now looks at life differently but deems himself in love with his career, his daughter (who is his biggest inspiration and what he is most thankful for) and his lady. He lives with his girlfriend in Caracas, Venezuela when he is not traveling. When he is at home with free time on his hands, he plays football and dominoes plus goes skateboarding. Mr. Hernandez likes all fruits and vegetables and he tries to eat a balanced diet, he also enjoys cooking rice and making salads. When asked what his Favourite book is, the reply was Reggae y Rastafari: Dos Formas De Entender El Caribe by Juan David Chacon. He wants to graduate from high school of music then continue his music studies to give his best to his daughter and his family.

Afro D

The Russian Reggae Pioneer

With one glance of Igor Diaknov, music fans are forced to re-imagine what they think a reggae artist should look like. The artist known as Afro D was not born on an island, in fact the Soviet Union. An acoustic guitar playing, singer/songwriter/ producer were deprived music from outside the USSR until his home land became the Russian Federation. From that point forward, music and Igor Diaknov would never be the same. He remembered the first foreign music his father

liked to play all day long. Such groups as Dire Straits, Queen, AC/DC and remember the first time he watched MTV with Michael Jackson videos, and also remember Ini Kamoze, "Here comes the hot Stepper". A son of a drummer and student of music, Afro D was born February 1, 1987 with

rhythm in his bones, and despite the fact that he was born outside the reggae capital of the world (Jamaica), this brethren exudes all that a reggae artist and a lover of Jah should be, through lyrical content and expression.

Afro D grew up in Moscow, USSR, where hard times and poverty did not pass him over. As eldest of his parent's three children, Afro D is no stranger to the pressure of hard times. He stated "It wasn't easy, from the age of 4, I have always been in the streets, sometimes it was rough, we played in a yard and watched the older boys, all addicted to heroin and toxic glue. Lots of their parents were alcoholics and had no job. They try to get that paycheck from the government. Others worked in factories twelve hours a day for little money. I have two younger sisters and it's not easy to be the older brother, believe me. My father wasn't so interested in our upbringing; he gave me advice very seldom. I spend time getting advice, because he was forever busy with trying to earn money but my mother helped me through childhood. I remember the lines of people who try to buy food by the card, sometimes you would have to wait three or more hours to get your meal. But my parents were always kind to me and give me all that they could give". These experiences have granted Afro D genuine humility and gratitude.

"People who are hurting, financially, emotionally and ill, inspirers me to do noble deed, so when I am asked to do a performance for free to help give back, I don't think about it, I just do it. I'm most thankful for my parents and god who gave me a chance to live this life, also gave me intellect to understand what's happening in this world. I'm thankful for I am not just a consumer or vampire, I can create something and share it with the world. And also I'm happy that I never have regrets."

Afro D's passion for life, transfers into his passion for reggae music and its culture, vice versa; in essence, life is reggae music and reggae music is life. Afro D strayed away from his native tongue and decided to record his music using English and Jamaican patois lyrics in order to reach a broader audience and authenticate his brand of reggae music. This transition was made permanent, and since then Afro D has performed at hundreds of venues. Mid 2010 Afro D began recording his first debut album "The First Step". It was around this same time he began working with the first Russian reggae background band, "The Stereo Drop". In 2011 "The Stereo Drop" organized weekly live reggae events call "Rocking Time" where Afro D was the special guest. In January 2012, Afro D released his first video "See Di Light", which was shot during the 100,000 man protest action against President Vladimir Putin, a testament to Afro D's impact as a musical and political revolutionary. The year 2013 was very successful for Afro D. He performed at the "Music for Bob 2013" in Moscow – international reggae festival, and shared the scene alongside Tippa Irie, Solo Banton and Radikal Guru. In April of that same year, Afro D made his voyage to Negril, where he was hailed and respected as one of the first Russian artists who truly compre-hend Jamaican and reggae culture.

On the 31st of May, 2013, Afro D's debut album "The First Step" was released in its fullness, featuring Mark Wonder (from Jamaica), Dub Unit (UK, Portugal), Jahsenda (Ghana), Maasto Records (Finland), Rebelsteppa (Russia), and Daniel Man (Russia). Along with mixing and mastering by Yuri "Der Circus" Markov. Ultimately, 1500 copies were released in CD (digi pack) and the album has been available for free download since its release. Afro D completed 2013 by shooting music video in Vietnam, a reggae love ballad, dedicated to his wife, entitled, "Darling". Afro D said "I have the best wife in the world. She is very intelligent and wise; she understands my way of life. She's the most beautiful girl I have ever met. She is not only my lover but also my best friend. One cannot build a good family based only on "sex"... a good relationship is based on friendship, love, understanding among other superb ingredients those are the secret."

Now in 2014, radio stations have begun to play Afro D's songs and dubs with regularity, Randy's Radio (New York), Ras Dave Show and Pulsar Radio (France), Culture Dub Show. In addition to Afro D's new secular buzz, he has released two smash singles, "Nah Believe" featuring Papa Lion (Russia), produced by Rebelsteppa and also "Family" which is the first Russian dancehall, music video featuring Luna T, and produced by El Toro. The "Family" video featured some of the best Russian dancehall teams.

In February 2014 he performed abroad for the first time with Jahneral Sound and Bass Sheriff Sound in Brno, and Boscovice (Czech Republic, the video was shot in Prague, "The Way of Righteousness" which was released in May 2014.

He performed with "The Dusters" a Russian reggae backing band at the Moscow Reggae Festival (vi) for the first time in May 2014. Also Afro D tunes were played on Riddim Roots Radio (UK) and had a big interview about reggae music in Russia alongside Farda Concious

In August 2014 he released a song "Never Get Dirty" on Freedom Riddim VA complication (Zona Reggae Music, Romania). Afro D also collaborated with Dub Phonic Netlabel (Cyprus) while doing monthly events with "The Dubsters" called "Heavyweight Dub Party."

Afro D's recent success is a culmination of his hard work, his dedication to creating authentic reggae music and the support he receives from his family and friends; their loyalty keeps this Russian reggae pioneer grounded and motivated. Afro D states "there are many people with whom I am close with, that always support my music. It would be dishonest if I say that one of them is the biggest supporter. I can tell one thing, my life became better, when I met my wife Polyna Diakonova, and a short list of people who I can call my best friends: Igor and Roma Arnaut, Mike Emishev, Alex Nikolaev, Konstantin Peshenko, Andrew Surovtsev –Butov (my friends from the block), Dmitry "Mc Dj adaj" Rum (reggae artist), Yuri"derCircus" Markov (my sound producer), and "The Stereo Drop" (reggae band)."

Afro D's passion, drive and genuine love for reggae music has him a pioneer of reggae in Russia and with his seamless transition to Jamaican patois lyrics, his fan base, along with his popularity is sprouting exponentially. Afro D has undoubtedly brought Russia into the reggae family.

****The following is Afro D's personal story,
as written by the artist himself***

Afro D's Journey

When I was young, I never thought and never dreamed to be a musician or singer. Once one completes music school that's a huge accomplishment and that was the moment my mother asked me "hey son, don't you want to play an instrument or maybe sing? My answer was: "No Maam," I love basketball and I want to be like 'Michael Jordan.' My godfather was one of the first in Moscow, to start playing reggae music. His band was called "Island", but that didn't matter to me much during that time. My world changed considerably, when I started to spend time in our home in the countryside. I was 15 playing the computer and listening music in the headphones, unaware of the storm brewing, when suddenly I felt a 'Bang' in my head out of nowhere, electricity traveled through my entire body. I was shocked, was frightened, because I didn't comprehend what had just happened to me. The thunder struck the electrical system because we have no lighting conductor? After a few days I felt better and at first my idea was maybe I became a superhero (laughing), I then found an old soviet acoustic guitar and tried to play it. I spent all of my summer holidays learning how to play various songs and from that day onward, music never left my head, it was like a mini radio, even in my sleep it was there. After a few years I started to write my own songs. All of which were in my native language. I played different genre of music, from Russian ballads, foreign rock, blues and many more. I performed with my first punk rock band as a singer and rhythm guitar.

At 18 I went to music school for a few years, there I met my best friend who introduced me to reggae music. I remember it as though it was only yesterday, because we always listened strictly to hip hop and rap music. My friend began to read a lot of books and information on the Rastafarian culture while at his flat he was listening to Bob Marley.

He asks me "what you think about it?" I answered "This music sounds sweet, I like when it sounds ruff." I fell in love with reggae music the moment I heard it. I didn't have internet at that time so I had to listen to Cd's and tapes, I don't quite remember who gave the CD's to me but they were amazing. Later I found different artists such as, Sizzla, Anthony B, Capleton, Junior Kelly, they sound rough which I liked, but I couldn't imagine that it was reggae music, for in my opinion it was some 'Strange Rap'. After this, the border between rap and reggae was broken and all I listen to was reggae CD's that my friend had.

When my family was able to afford the internet, my life changed in an enormous way, for I was able to bury myself more in a world of reggae music. It was then that I began to write my first three reggae songs in Russian and recorded them. I then found out that I was not alone, for there were others in my town that loved and wanted reggae music in their social communities. I found about 10 people and created my first reggae band. That was my first success on my music journey. We performed at various festivals and solo concerts, but our music was far from actual reggae music, this was because not all musicians are capable of feeling the vibes, riddim and zing of reggae music.

I left college at 21 to pursue my love and passion for music, but as one grows older; they come to the realization that they need real money for living and our music wasn't cutting it. I became frustrated with seeking new musicians who had the zest, passion and could play reggae music like I did without mixing it with fun or rock music. Sometimes, I had nothing to eat and my friends and relatives would help by pitching in where they could. During this same period I also discovered digital riddims, downloaded hundreds of versions from the whole world and chanting and singing on them alone, that's when it dawned on me that I didn't need a group to be a reggae artist or to perform live. I decided to start my own carrier. I began to meet a lot of Russian promoters of reggae music, I worked along with those artist, sound producers and selectors as we worked together to build the first reggae Russian label. We built our own recording studio, worked together as a promo group; we organized and perform in weekly and daily events.

We supported each other in recording sessions and promotion. "One for all and all for one," we all wrote self-representing lyrics and also dancehall lyrics. My influences were, Sean Paul, Shaggy, Shabba, Mavado and Vybz Cartel. Dancehall music became popular in Moscow, which spread like wild fyah burning all across the country. But unfortunately, we looked more like youthful maximalists, not the real thing. During this time, we believed that reggae could be "adopted" for Russian lyrics, but after a while, as I was listening to the sounds of the Jamaican music, my Russian lyrics were paled. I went as far as doing my first steps in English then in patois, I became enchanted so much that I read tons of books about Jamaica, patois, the culture, I discovered so much, even got hooked on some new tunes and artists.

My taste in music changed enormously, I began to write the lyrics for my first album. I soon found a producer who could write excellent rhythm right in Moscow, I was advised to connect with foreign reggae musicians in order to network. Soon I met my old fellows from "The Stereo Drop" we performed together with my first band. Then drummer of the band left, so the decided to change the name of the group to 'Back Ground Band.' They knew just a few Jamaican riddims some riddims which they arranged by themselves. I had about 14 songs and we decided to work with my material and perform together. It was an amazing feeling. Danila, the new band member advises me to work with Yuri Markov, a producer. We released my album "Big Tings a Gwaan" featuring musicians from around the world and two videos which received 40,000 views on YouTube. Today, I love music from Sugar Minott, Gentleman and Alborosie, who shows people that you don't need to be a Jamaican to sing reggae music, but you must be wise, work hard, dedication and nothing comes easy. As they say in Jamaica, 'if you really want good, your nose affy run.'

I love different authors and books, which changes ones perspective of life on a whole that gives me new experiences. I can recall one of these books by Phillip Sudo called 'Zen Guitar,' when reading this book it taught me that "One must put all of their energy and spirit into life". It's a very small book but extremely informative, each time I read it, I learn something in my music journey. I love to read poems by Mayakovsky and books by Hanter Thompson. Richard Bakh also changed my lifestyle, his books taught me, that everything and anything is possible. Last book I read was by Beth Lesser "Rub-a-Dub Style," "The Roots of Modern Dancehall" a great guide to understanding Jamaican culture.

I am abhorrent when people do fake music, in the sense of music without soul and only done for money. Don't get me wrong we have to make money with our skills and talents but do so with some pride without selling out oneself. In my country most of music is fake, there are a few that make true music. I can honestly say that I dislike when people lie to themselves and in most cases we are looked upon by those as role models, but what example are we truly trying to show to those who look up to us when we lie to ourselves so frequently. I am drawn to creativity in others especially with their superb imagination; all musicians are like brothers and sisters to me.

I want to find a serene and comfortable place to live and not worry about how to survive. Russia is a rough country; we have huge numerous and enormous problems with corruption and 'poli-tricks'. I have an assortment of goals that I want to accomplish. I want to better formulate my sound, my lyrics, my skills and the quality of my music videos. Each song I write is my favorite, because they were all written in a different period in my life. "HG" featuring Mark Wonder from Kingston, Jamaica, is very special to me. It was my first experience of working with Jamaican artists, and Mark is still one of my favourite singers, of roots and culture. Reggae music for me is superior. In reggae you will find an answer to any question, 'Reggae' in itself is like a universal cure and love to perform with a live band. We are trying to play original reggae music, not mix with any different styles, we have all imagined that we are Jamaicans at one point or another, it's funny but true, but we can't stop doing it. Without a muse to inspire creation or creativity, life is simply meaningless. We need to appreciate more, forgive quickly, love and live in the moment of 'reggae'.

Special Thank You

Center Stage Dance Academy, thank you for the donations.

Crystal & Family thank you for the donations.

Christopher, you have been a great support and help. Thank you for your love and support.

Cindy, thank you for the donations.

Brianna Charlton, thank you so very much for your help with the book.

Jennifer Elvyn, my beautiful grandmother if it was not for you I would not have known who my great-great grandfather Granville Campbell was Jamaica's first classical & love singer.

Kairi Jamar Suswell, thank you so very much for your help with the book.

Lonette, my best friend you went above and beyond to help make my first book and charity event a success. Thank you for your loving support.

Mrs. Hopkin 5th grade class at Willow Dale Elementary School invited me to speak about what it's like to be an author. Thank you, for being my first public speaking class.

Sally Simons, thank you so very much for your help with the book.

Willow Dale Elementary School, thank you for the donations.

Nicolette & Natalia my beautiful daughters, thank you for giving me strength. Mommy loves you both.

Nyema Gordon

To: Ms. Dennis

We thank you for the effort
And all your support
We also thank you for your love
Your heart is just flying
High as a dove.
We thank you for these stationeries
We will use them carefully
All you have to give is from your heart
Nothing can stop your love after it starts
You are a very generous lady
May God Bless you continually.

5th Grader at Eccleston Primary School in St. Ann, Jamaica

Apart

There was a time that I once knew
when it was only me and you.
The world we had was a silent step
to the memories we had kept.
I miss you too much and will always know
that I could never let you go.
I hope one day we'll be together and
when we are, it will be forever.
Our love will be our guiding light
until we meet on that special night.

In memory of Wesley Elvyn, my Grandfather AKA Champs,
June 5th 1937 to July 12th 2014

Photo Credits

Black Prophet	Warren Millar
David Dinsmore	Mike McGrath, Jimmy Iles, and Rod Tanaka
Da'Ville	Kali McCrathy, and Gail Zucker,
Dax Lion	Daniel Savage
Jah Lex	Alexandria Gayle
Mikey Dangerous	Felix Rioux and Dan Mathieu
Paul Anthony	Maria Bartosh
Richie Campbell	Pedro Dias
Tony Curtis	Debo Photo Studio
Uwe Banton	Gail Zucker, Lisa Jung, and Max Strasser

CPSIA information can be obtained
at www.ICGtesting.com
Printed in the USA
BVHW091021040419
544608BV00016B/138/P